Problems of Im
studies critical and

Joseph Warschauer

Alpha Editions

This edition published in 2024

ISBN 9789362513014

Design and Setting By
Alpha Editions
www.alphaedis.com
Email - info@alphaedis.com

As per information held with us this book is in Public Domain.
This book is a reproduction of an important historical work.
Alpha Editions uses the best technology to reproduce historical work
in the same manner it was first published to preserve its original nature.
Any marks or number seen are left intentionally to preserve.

Contents

PREFACE	- 1 -
INTRODUCTION DIVINE IMMANENCE	- 4 -
CHAPTER I SOME PROBLEMS OF IMMANENCE	- 10 -
CHAPTER II PANTHEISM: THE SUICIDE OF RELIGION	- 19 -
CHAPTER III THE ETHICS OF MONISM	- 25 -
CHAPTER IV MONISM AND THE INDIVIDUAL	- 31 -
CHAPTER V THE DIVINE PERSONALITY	- 36 -
CHAPTER VI	- 43 -
CHAPTER VII	- 50 -
CHAPTER VIII THE DENIAL OF EVIL	- 59 -
NOTE.	- 67 -
CHAPTER IX DETERMINISM	- 71 -
CHAPTER X MORALITY AS A RELIGION	- 86 -
CHAPTER XI PROBLEMS OF PRAYER	- 97 -
CHAPTER XII IMMORTALITY	- 110 -

PREFACE

About a year ago certain tendencies in the popular discussion of the doctrine of Divine Immanence suggested to the present writer the idea of a brief sketch or article, to be published under the title, "The Truth of Transcendence." On further reflection, however, a somewhat more extended treatment of so important a subject seemed desirable, and this has been attempted in the following chapters. When the doctrine of immanence began, as it has been of late, to be reasserted in a somewhat pronounced manner, most of those who were best able to judge felt conscious of certain dangers likely to arise through misinterpretation and over-emphasis; that those anticipations have been abundantly realised, no careful student of recent developments will dispute, and the present book is intended both to call attention to these dangers and to bring out the distinction between the truth of immanence and what to the author seem perversions of that truth.

In the meantime, while these pages were passing through the press, there has appeared a new work from the brilliant pen of Professor William James,[1] some sentences from which might to a large extent be taken as indicating the standpoint of the volume now submitted to the reader:—

"God," in the religious life of ordinary men is the name not of the whole of things, heaven forbid, but only of the ideal tendency in things, believed in as a superhuman person who calls us to co-operate in His purposes, and who furthers ours if they are worthy. He works in an external environment, has limits, and has enemies. When John Mill said that the notion of God's omnipotence must be given up, if God is to be kept as a religious object, he was surely accurately right; yet, so prevalent is the lazy Monism that idly haunts the regions of God's name, that so simple and truthful a saying was generally treated as a paradox; God, it was said, *could* not be finite. I believe that the only God worthy of the name *must* be finite.

It is precisely the theory which identifies God with "the whole of things" which will be combated in the following discussions; it is precisely "the lazy Monism that idly haunts the regions of God's name" to which they offer a plain and direct challenge. At the same time such a phrase as that in which Professor James speaks of God as working "in an external environment" would seem unduly to under-emphasise the fact of immanence; and it may be said at once that the theory of Divine finitude put forward by the present writer will be seen to differ from that of John Stuart Mill, as the idea of *self*-limitation differs from that of a limitation *ab extra*—in other words, as Theism differs from Deism.

It is perhaps a little remarkable that the fundamental antinomies which arise from the assumption of the actual infinity of God should not have been more frequently dealt with; or rather, that thinkers postulating that infinity as a basal axiom should have been comparatively blind to its logical implications. For if God is infinite, then He is all; and if He is all, what becomes of human individuality, or how are human initiative and responsibility so much as thinkable? Benjamin Jowett, in his Essay on Predestination and Freewill, glanced at this problem in passing, and the remarks he made upon it more than fifty years ago, if somewhat tentative, are well worth consideration to-day:—

"God is infinite." But in what sense? . . . Press the idea of the infinite to its utmost extent, till it is alone in the universe, or rather is the universe itself, in this heaven of abstraction, nevertheless, a cloud begins to appear; a limitation casts its shadow over the formless void. Infinite is finite because it is infinite. That is to say, because infinity includes all things, it is incapable of creating what is external to itself. Deny infinity in this sense, and the being to whom it is attributed receives a new power. *God is greater by being finite than by being infinite* . . . Logic must admit that the infinite over-reaches itself by denying the existence of the finite, and that there are some "limitations," such as the impossibility of evil or falsehood, which are of the essence of the Divine nature.[2]

Where, of course, Divine immanence is held to mean the "allness"—which is the strict equivalent of the infinity—of God, evil in every shape and form will either have to be ascribed to the direct will and agency of God Himself, or for apologetic purposes to be reduced to a mere semblance, or "not-being." Thus we are told to-day in plain terms that "if God does not avert evil, it is because He requires it"; that "what to us seems evil is ordained of God"; that—

"If prayers and earthquakes break not Heaven's design,
How then a Borgia or a Catiline?"

But if evil be only apparent and not real, we shall surely, having gained this insight, be too wise to waste indignation upon the non-existent; if what we call misdeeds in reality fulfil God's own "requirements," a thoroughly enlightened public opinion will not seek to interfere with the sacred activities of the pick-pocket, the forger, the sweater, the *roué*, every one of whom may plead that he is but carrying out the Divine ordinances; if Alexander Borgia's perjuries, poisonings and debaucheries "break not Heaven's design," but are "ordained of God for some purpose," morality itself becomes an exploded anachronism.

It is because these and such as these are the results in the fields of religion and conduct which flow from certain errors in the field of speculation, that these chapters have been written, and are now sent forth. Belief in a personal God, personal freedom, personal immortality—these essentials of religion are one and all endangered where the doctrine of Divine immanence is presented in terms of a monistic philosophy; it has been the writer's object to safeguard and vindicate these truths anew in a volume which, though of necessity largely critical in method, he offers as wholly constructive in aim.

August 1st, 1909.

[1] *A Pluralistic Universe.*

[2] *Thessalonians, Galatians and Romans,* vol. ii. pp. 388-9.

INTRODUCTION
DIVINE IMMANENCE

The doctrine of Divine immanence is in a very special and unmistakeable manner the re-discovery of the nineteenth century. Nothing could be more remote from fact than to call that doctrine a new—or even an old—heresy. Old it certainly is, but heretical in itself it as certainly is not; it can point to unquestionable warranty in Holy Scripture, where such is demanded, and it has never been repudiated by the Christian Church. But just as a law, without being repealed, may fall into desuetude, so a doctrine, without being repudiated, may for a time fade out of the Church's consciousness; and in the one case as in the other any attempt at revival will arouse a certain amount of distrust and opposition. There would no doubt be a measure of truth in the statement that the suspicion and antagonism with which the recent re-enunciation of this particular doctrine or idea was attended in some quarters, exemplified this general attitude of the human mind towards the unaccustomed; and yet such a statement, made without qualification, would be only a half-truth. The fact is, and it cannot be stated too soon or too clearly, that if the antagonism and suspicion exhibited have been exceptionally strong, there have been exceptional causes to justify both. Alarm, and that of a very legitimate nature, has been called forth by one-sided and extravagant statements of the idea of Divine immanence on the part of ill-balanced advocates; and in this book we shall be almost continually occupied with the task of disengaging the truth of immanence from what appear to us mischievous travesties of that truth. That such a task is a necessary one, we are firmly convinced; for if, as Principal Adeney says, "among all the changes in theology that have been witnessed during the last hundred years this"—*i.e.*, the re-discovery of the principle of Divine immanence—"is the greatest, the most revolutionary," it must certainly be of paramount importance that we should understand and apply that principle aright. Confessedly, it denotes a great and far-reaching change; can we, then, in the first instance, briefly and plainly state what this change is from, what it involves, and in what respect it is supposed to help us in dealing with the problem of religion?

It has to be borne in mind, to begin with, that the very term "immanence" had for a long time ceased to be in current use, and had thus become strange to the average believer; it has equally to be remembered that in theology as in other matters we have not yet altogether passed the stage where *hostis* means both "stranger" and "foe"—that, in fact, to many minds, the unfamiliar is, as we said, *eo ipso* the suspect. But immanence means nothing more abstruse than "indwelling"; and the renewed emphasis which, from the time of Wordsworth onward, began to be laid upon the Divine indwelling, the presence of God in the Universe, represented in the first place the reaction of the human spirit against the cold and formal Deism of the eighteenth century, which thought of God as remote, external to the world, exclusively "transcendent." According to the deistic notion, God was known to man only by reason of a revelation He had given once and for all in the far-off past—a revelation which in its very nature excluded the idea of progress; as against this conception that of the immanence of God declares that He is not far from each one of us, that in Him we live and move and have our being, that He is over all and through all and in all—the Life of all life, the Energy behind all phenomena, the Presence from which there is no escaping, unceasingly and progressively—though by divers portions and in divers manners—revealed in the universe, in nature and in man.

Thus expressed, the doctrine of God's nearness and indwelling will probably commend itself to most thoughtful religious people; but in re-emphasising an aspect of truth there is always the danger of over-emphasising it, of claiming it as the whole and sole truth—of falling, in a word, from one extreme into the other. To that rule the present case offers no exception; it is, on the contrary, very distinctly one of the pendulum swinging as far in one direction as it previously swung to the other. Let us then at once state the thesis which many of the following pages will serve to elaborate: when the *indwelling* of God in the universe is interpreted as meaning His *identity* with the universe; when the *indwelling* of God in man is taken to mean His *identity* with man, the whole structure of religion is gravely imperilled. For in the identity of God with the world and with man—which is the root-tenet of Pantheism—there is inevitably involved the surrender of both the Divine and the human personality. We shall have occasion to see how much such a surrender signifies; for the moment it suffices to say plainly that Pantheism, the doctrine which denies the transcendence of God, is by no means the same as that which affirms His immanence, nor does it logically follow from that affirmation. The mistake so frequently made lies in regarding the Divine immanence and the Divine transcendence as mutually exclusive alternatives, whereas they are complementary to one another. A one-sided insistence on the immanence of God, to the exclusion of His transcendence, leads to Pantheism, just as a one-sided insistence upon His transcendence, to the exclusion of His immanence, leads to Deism; it is the two taken together that result in, and are necessary to, Theism. Thus it cannot be too well understood, and it should be understood at the very outset, that we have not to make anything like a choice between immanence and transcendence—that these two can never be separated, but are related to each other as the less to the greater, as the part to the whole. One naturally shrinks from employing a diagram in dealing with such a topic as this; but perhaps recourse might without offence be had to this method—necessarily imperfect as it is—on account of its essential simplicity, and because it is calculated to remove misapprehensions. If we can think of a very large sphere, A, and, situated anywhere *within* this, of a very small sphere, a—then the relation of the smaller to the greater will be that of the sphere of immanence to the sphere of transcendence. The two are not mutually separable, but the one has its being wholly within the other.

Nevertheless it is quite true that there has been within recent years a distinct shifting of the centre of gravity from the one doctrine to the other, a growing disposition to regard the immanence of God as the fundamental datum, the basis of the modern restatement of religious belief. How will this conception help us to such an end? The answer to that question may be given in the words of Dr. Horton, who says, "The intellectual background of our time is Agnosticism, and *the reply which faith makes to Agnosticism is couched in terms of the immanence of God.*" [1] Dr. Horton's meaning will grow clearer to us if we once more glance at our imaginary diagram, letting the smaller figure a, the sphere of immanence, stand for our universe. If the sphere of God's being lay altogether outside the universe, *i.e.*, outside the radius of our knowledge—if He, in other words, were merely and altogether transcendent—He would also be merely and altogether unknowable, exactly as Agnosticism avers. His transcendent attributes, all that partakes of infinity, cannot—and that of necessity—become objects of immediate knowledge to finite minds; if He is to be known at all to us, He can only be so known by being manifested through His presence within, or action upon, the finite and comprehensible sphere. In other words, *it is primarily as He is revealed in and through the finite world, that is to say as immanent, that God becomes knowable to us*; all that is included under His transcendence is of the very highest importance for us—religion would be utterly incomplete without it—but it is an inference we make from His immanence. It is, to give an obvious illustration, only to a transcendent God that we can offer prayer—God over all whom the soul needs, to enter into relations withal; but it is also true that we gain the assurance of His transcendence through His immanence, and that

> The God without he findeth not,
>   Who finds Him not within.

In a word, the Divine immanence is not the goal of our quest of God, but it is the indispensable starting-point.

A simple reflection will serve to place this beyond doubt. Against the old-fashioned Deism which continued to bear sway till far into the last century, the agnostic had an almost fatally easy case; he had but to reject the revelation alleged to have been given once for all in the dim past—to reject it on scientific or critical grounds—and who was to prove to him that the universe had been created a few thousand years ago by a remote and external Deity? As for him, he professed, and professed candidly enough, that he could see nothing in nature but the operation of impersonal forces; there was natural law, and there was the process of evolution, but beyond these———? Now the only really telling reply that can be made to those who argue in this fashion is that which reasons from the Divine immanence as its *terminus a quo*—the doctrine which beholds God first of all present and active *in* the world, and sees in natural law not a possible substitute for Him, but the working of His sovereign Will. From this point of view, the orderliness of the cosmos, the uniformity and regularity of nature, attest not the unconscious throbbing of a soulless engine, or a blind Power behind phenomena, but a directing Mind, a prevailing Will. The world, according to this conception, was not "made" once upon a time, like a piece of clockwork, and wound up to run without further assistance; it is not a mechanism, but an organism, thrilled and pervaded by an eternal Energy that "worketh even until now." In Sir Oliver Lodge's phrase, we must look for the action of Deity, if at all, then always; and this thought of the indwelling God, revealing Himself in the majestic course and order of nature, not only rebuts the assaults of Agnosticism, but compels our worship. And as natural law speaks to us of the steadfastness and prevailing power of the Divine Will, so evolution speaks of the Divine Purpose, and proclaims that purpose "somehow good," since evolution means a steady reaching forward and upward, an unfolding and ascent from less to more.

We take a step higher up when we come to the further revelation of God as seen dwelling in man; a step higher up because on any sane view immanence is a fact admitting of very various degrees, so that God is more fully revealed in the organic than in the inorganic world, more in the conscious than in the unconscious, far more in man than in lower creatures. We speak of God's indwelling in man in the same sense in which there is something of an earthly parent's very being in his children; indeed, rightly considered, the Divine Parenthood is the only rational guarantee of that human brotherhood which is being so strongly—or, at least, so loudly—insisted on to-day. Man, that is to say, is not identical with God, any more than a son is identical with his father; but man is consubstantial, homogeneous, with God, lit by a Divine spark within him, a partaker of the Divine substance. As in nature we discern God revealed as Power, Mind, Will, Purpose, so in man's moral nature, and his inner satisfaction or dissatisfaction according as he does or does not approach a certain moral standard, we discern Him as Righteousness; and, more than all, since men, beings in whom "the Spirit of God dwelleth," are persons, it follows that

God also is at least personal, since there can be nothing in an effect that is not in the cause producing it. Thus the doctrine of Divine immanence throws at least a ray of light upon one of the problems which press with peculiar weight upon many modern minds—and which we shall consider at greater length hereafter—*viz.*, the Divine Personality.

There remains, however, a still further step to be taken along the line which we have been pursuing. We are not fully satisfied when we know God even as personal, even as righteous; the assurance which alone will satisfy the awakened human spirit is that which tells us that God is Love, and that His truest name is that of Father. How could such a culminating assurance come to us? We conceive that this end could only be achieved through a complete manifestation of the Divine character on a finite scale, *i.e.*, through His indwelling in an unparalleled measure in a unique and ethically perfect being; and such an event, we hold, has actually taken place in what is known as the Incarnation. In the words of Dr. Horton, "the doctrine of the immanence of God, the idea that God is in us all, leads us irresistibly to the conclusion that 'God was in Christ, reconciling the world unto Himself.'" "This argument," he says—*viz.*, from Divine immanence—"becomes more and more favourable to the doctrine of Christ's Divinity." [2] The highest and truest knowledge of God, that which it most concerns us to possess, could have become ours only through One in whom the fulness of Godhead dwelt bodily, in whom we saw Divinity in its essence and without alloy. To bring us this perfect revelation was, indeed, the very reason of Christ's advent. We come to the Father through the Son, because there is no other Way. We have seen the light of the knowledge of the glory of God in the face of Jesus Christ, the very Image of His Substance. Divine Love, mighty to save, full of redemptive power, longing for the soul with infinite affection—in fine, Fatherhood—this is what constitutes religion's ultimate; and this revelation we have in the Incarnate Son, in whom the Spirit dwelt without measure—who, *i.e.*, stands forth as the supreme and unparalleled illustration of the Divine immanence.

Here, then, we have a first, preliminary survey of the meaning of this much-discussed, much-misunderstood term—a mere outline sketch which, needless to say, requires a great deal of filling in, such as will be attempted in subsequent pages of this book. So much should be clear from what has been said, that the nineteenth century, in practically restoring this fruitful and far-reaching conception to a Church which had largely forgotten it, made a contribution of the utmost importance to theology and religion; indeed, the value of that contribution could hardly be more strongly stated than in the utterances of Dr. Horton which we have quoted above. Such a factor, however, cannot be introduced, or re-introduced, into our theological thinking without necessitating a good deal of revision, nor without causing a certain measure of temporary confusion and dislocation; it will accordingly be the principal object of the following chapters to clear up misapprehensions which have arisen in connection with the idea of immanence, to assign to it its approximately proper place in Christian thought, and to safeguard an important truth against the injury done to it—and so to all truth—by a zeal that is not according to knowledge. *Corruptio optimi pessima*: in unskilled hands this doctrine is certainly apt to become a danger to religion itself; nevertheless, rightly applied, there is probably no more potent instrument than this to help us in that reconstruction of belief which is admittedly the urgent business of our age. It is true, as Raymond Brucker said, that "the answer to the riddle of the universe is God—the answer to the riddle of God is Christ"; but it is also true, we hold, that the most effective key for the unlocking of the riddle is the idea of Divine immanence.

[1] *My Belief*, p. 107.

[2] *Op. cit.*; pp. 108, 109.

CHAPTER I
SOME PROBLEMS OF IMMANENCE

It used to be said of a famous volume of apologetics—with what justification this is not the place to discuss—that it raised more difficulties than it professed to settle; and a somewhat similar charge has more than once been brought against the doctrine of Divine immanence, *viz.*, that if it succeeded in throwing light upon some problems, it created new ones of a particularly insoluble character. The old deistic notion which interposed a distance between the Creator and His creation, and in particular represented God as *there* and man as *here*, might be untenable in philosophy, but it was at least intelligible and practically helpful to ordinary minds; but does not the idea of God's immanence in the world and in man tend to efface that distinction, and thus to introduce confusion where confusion is least to be desired?

In the present chapter we shall attempt to glance at some of the main questions which arise in connection with this doctrine; and, to begin with, we may state with the utmost frankness that nothing is easier than to interpret the conception of Divine immanence in such a manner as to make it appear either ludicrous or hateful or simply meaningless—in any case repulsive from the religious point of view. This, to come straight to the point, is what is bound to happen when God's indwelling in man is explained as meaning that man is *de facto* one with his Maker. What could the general reader think when he was told with vehemence, "You are yourself the infinite"—"You are yourself God; you never were anything else"? If that reader was lacking in mental balance, he was likely to be swept off his feet by such a declaration, and to accept, with all its implications, a view so flattering to human vanity; if, on the other hand, he was a person of soberly religious outlook and experience, he inquired what was the doctrine in whose name such a proposition was offered to him for acceptance—and on learning that the name of that doctrine was the unfamiliar one of "immanence," straightway set it down as the worst of brain-sick heresies. Thus, not for the first time, has a cause or truth been wounded and discredited by injudicious advocacy.

For the purpose which we have in view we cannot do better than state what we consider the fundamental misinterpretation of this doctrine in the considered words of one of its most popular exponents, who expresses it as follows: "God *in* man is God *as* man. There is no real Divine Immanence which does not imply the allness of God." [1] It is not too much to say that this brief statement contains the *fons et origo* of all the misunderstandings with which the re-enunciation of this idea has been attended; it is this assumption of the allness of God which underlies and colours quite a number of modern movements, and will be seen to lead those who accept it into endless and inextricable tangles.

If God is all, *then what are we?* Granted the basal axiom of this type of immanentism, it follows with irresistible cogency that our separate existence, consciousness, volitions and so forth are merely illusions. We can be "ourselves God" only in the sense that we are individually nothing; the contrary impression is simply an error, which we shall have to recognise as such, and to get rid of with what speed and thoroughness we can. This, it is true, is more easily said than done, for our whole life both of thought and action bears incessant witness to the opposite; there are, however, those to whose temperament such a complete contradiction, so far from being distressing, is positively grateful because of its suggestion of mystery and mysticism. Sometimes a Tertullian voices this abdication of the reasoning faculty defiantly—*certum est quia impossibile est*; but more often perhaps the same position is expressed in the spirit of Tennyson's well-known lines, which, indeed, bear directly upon our immediate theme:—

> We feel we are nothing—for all is Thou and in Thee;
> We feel we are something—*that* also has come from Thee;
> We know we are nothing—but Thou wilt help us to be.

We submit, however, that while such a contemplation of, or oscillation between, mutually destructive tenets may for a time minister to some kind of aesthetic enjoyment, the healthy mind cannot permanently find satisfaction while thus suspended in mid-air; nor are we appreciably advanced by the temper which, after pointing out some alleged fundamental antinomy, "quietly accepts"—*i.e.*, in practice ignores—it. Problems of this description are not solved by what Matthew Arnold called a want of intellectual seriousness; is it true, we ask, that the "mystical view of the Divine immanence" compels us to believe in the allness of God, and so to deny our individual existence?

The answer is that this *soi-disant* "mystical view" is simply a distorted view of what immanence means. We are not really called upon to do violence to the collective facts of our experience, which rise up in unanimous and spontaneous testimony against the monstrous fiction that we are either nothing or God. The fallacy upon which this fiction rests is not a very subtle one. When we speak of God's indwelling in man, we predicate that community of nature which the writer of Gen. ii expresses by saying that God created man in His own image; we predicate, *i.e.*, what we already called homogeneity—likeness of substance—and not identity, which is a very different thing. We do not commit ourselves to the proposition that

"God *in* man is God *as* man." Parent and child are linked together by a precisely analogous bond to that subsisting between God and man, but they are nevertheless distinct individualities.

"But," it will be objected, "the analogy does not hold, for parent and child are both finite; how can a similar separateness be so much as thought to exist between God and man, seeing that God is infinite?" It will be seen that the objection merely restates the allness of God under a different form; and this brings us to the very heart of the matter. We must at length face the one conclusion which does not land us in self-contradiction—*viz.*, that *in the act of creation God limits His own infinity*, no matter to how infinitesimal an extent. On the alternative supposition we have ultimately to think of God and man either as All *plus* something or All *plus* zero—which is absurd. Mr. Chesterton has rendered useful service by insisting that in creating the world God distinguishes Himself from the world, as a poet is distinct from his poem—a truth which he has condensed into an aphorism, "All creation is separation"; but on the part of the Deity such "separation" implies of necessity the self-limitation just spoken of. Just as a billion, *minus* the billionth fraction of a unit, is no longer a billion, so infinity itself, limited though it be but by a hair's-breadth, is no longer, strictly speaking, infinite. Once we admit this Divine self-limitation as a working theory, we shall no longer be troubled by the unreal difficulty of having to reconcile the principle of Divine immanence with the fact of individual existence. The Divine spark may burn in man, brightly or dimly as the case may be, and yet be separate from the central and eternal Fire whence it has been flung forth; in other words, man may be a partaker of the Divine nature without being "himself God." If we are to be able to believe in either a universe or a humanity which, though the scene of Divine immanence, are not identical with God, it seems to us that such a view of creation as we have just propounded is inevitable; and unless this non-identity can be maintained—unless, that is to say, we definitely repudiate the idea of the "allness" of God—religion itself is reduced to a misty and ineffective theosophy.

The issues involved in the acceptance or rejection of this view appear to us of such importance that, at the risk of seeming to labour our point unnecessarily, we are anxious to make it perfectly plain. In the phase through which religious thought is passing to-day there are few things more urgently needed than to dispel that interpretation of immanence which obliterates the line of demarcation between God and man. We may decline the mechanical dualism which placed the Creator altogether outside the universe, and yet embrace a view which for want of a better name might be called spiritual dualism, and which maintains the distinction of which we are speaking. What happens when that distinction is lost, is sufficiently apparent from a statement like the following, actually addressed to a miscellaneous audience: "If there is an eternal throne, you are on it now; there has never been a moment when you were not on it." Such downright extravagance is most suitably met with a bald contradiction: man is *not* on the eternal throne, and there has never been a moment when he was on it. It is this fact which makes worship so much as possible; it is, in short, the transcendent God with whom we are concerned in the exercise of religion, for as Mr. Chesterton puts it in his own manner, "that Jones shall worship the god within him turns out ultimately to mean that Jones shall worship Jones."

Let us see what follows if we once seriously persuade ourselves that we are "on the eternal throne," or, to extract its meaning from that picturesque phrase, that the presence of God is already perfectly realised in us. We cannot but think we shall carry the reader with us in saying that such a belief is in itself indicative of spiritual danger; indeed, there can hardly be a greater danger than that which is directly encouraged by the idea that we have already attained, and that all is well with us, seeing that we are one with the All-good. On such a supposition, why pray—for even were there One other than ourselves to pray to, what is there to pray for? Or, to quote the actual question of a believer in this kind of immanence, Why ask outside for a strength which we already possess? What a naïve question of this calibre reveals only too plainly is that self-complacency which is the most deadly foe of the spiritual life. One is reminded of the American story in which a bright and intelligent wife asks her cultured but indifferent husband, "Is it true that God is immanent in us all?" "I suppose so," he answers; "*but it does not greatly matter.*" The question is, Do we already possess the strength for which we ask? Or rather, Does not the very fact that we ask for it prove that we do not possess it, and that He from whom we ask it is not ourselves? Is not the gift of the Holy Spirit, the Divine invasion of the soul, a fact of experience, and is it not also a fact that that gift is only to be had for the asking, only given in response to earnest and persevering prayer, and that it effects in those who receive it a change of thought and feeling?

All these are facts resting on irrefragable evidence; the apparent problem is, to harmonise them with the affirmation of the divinity existing in man. If God be truly "in us all," then in what sense or to what purpose can we pray for a consummation which, it will be urged, is *ex hypothesi* an accomplished fact at the time that we ask for it? We reply that the Divine indwelling in man is of the nature of a capacity for striving rather than of an attainment, a potentiality rather than an actuality, a prophecy rather than a fulfilment. Man's longing for communion with God, as for an unrealised good, is the longing of like for Like, but it is only through struggle and effort that the goal can be reached. The Eternal is indeed the Life of all life, and to that extent it is true that all life expresses Him; nevertheless our original divine endowment is no more than the material which has to be shaped and wrought into "the type of perfect." Without this divinity of substance as it might be called, we should never have the finished product, divinity of character; but the latter can only be achieved through arduous and persevering endeavour. Without a genuinely divine element—without the Spirit breathed into man by his Creator—we could not even realise our failure, nor aspire after a fuller portion of that same life-giving Spirit; it is what we have that tells us of what we lack, and directs us to Him who alone can supply our want out of His inexhaustible fulness.

And if we have thus found an answer to the question, "How, from the point of view of Divine immanence, can there be anything but God?" we have at the same time received a hint indicating where we shall have to look for the answer to another query of even more directly practical interest, *viz.*, "How, from the same point of view, can there be anything but *good*—how can there be any real evil, physical or moral?" Put in that extreme form, this problem, like the one with which we have just dealt, arises from the erroneous assertion of the allness of God; but as the whole subject of the reality of evil will come up for treatment at a later stage, we need not now enter into its discussion. At one aspect, and one only, of this vast and complex theme we may, however, be permitted to glance for a moment before we pass on. If God dwells in us, it is frequently asked, whence comes what Paul so pathetically calls "the law of sin which is in our members"—whence come the wrongful desires and harmful passions of whose power we are so painfully conscious? That is an entirely legitimate and even inevitable query, but the solution of the enigma is not past finding out, though we must content ourselves with a mere suggestion. We have, in the first place to keep our hold of the fact, disregarding all pleas to the contrary, that sin is a reality, and not a phantasm of our imagination; we shall then diagnose its nature as the misuse, the unfaithful administration, of the power which God has conferred upon us for employment in His holy service; and then, lastly, we shall grow aware that the very pain, the sense of unhappiness and moral discord by which the consciousness of guilt is ever accompanied, is the protesting voice of that which is the deepest reality within ourselves—the indwelling Divine.

But when we have shown that the doctrine of Divine immanence does not, as some of its advocates would have us believe, swallow up human individuality—a subject to which we shall return—we are faced with yet another difficulty. The question is asked—again, quite naturally and inevitably—In what sense can we speak of God as immanent in the inorganic world? How, *e.g.*, does a stone embody or express His essence?— and yet, if it is not somehow a manifestation of Him, what is this cold, lifeless, ponderable substance we call a stone? Nor do matters grow simpler when we ascend in the scale: we may trace the immanent Deity in all that is good and fair in nature, in all its smiling and beneficent moods—but what of nature's uglinesses and cruelties? Is God expressing Himself in the ferocity of the tiger, the poisonous malice of the cobra, the greed of every unclean carrion-bird? If He is such as religion represents Him, how can He be present in these? We may quote with rapture the familiar lines in which the poet tells us:—

> I have felt
> A presence that disturbs me with the joy
> Of elevated thoughts...

But the world which is the dwelling of that something "far more deeply interfused" of which Wordsworth sings, does not consist exclusively of

> the light of setting suns,
> And the round ocean, and the living air,
> And the blue sky...

—it contains also dismal, fever-breeding swamps, dreadful deserts, dreary wastes of eternal ice, plunged into darkness half the year; are we going simply to ignore these realities when we speak of the Divine indwelling in the world? And, once more, shall we assert this doctrine when we remember the cold cunning of the spider, or the delight in torture displayed by the domestic cat?

It depends, we answer, what we mean by "this doctrine"; if we construe immanence to signify "allness," we may as well admit first as last that there is no way of escape from the difficulties which these queries suggest. In that case it is not for us to pick and choose—to say that God is the beauty of the beautiful, but not the ugliness of the ugly; the compassion of the compassionate, but not the cruelty of the cruel: if He is *all*, He is *both*, and for that very reason is *neither*. That is the real inwardness of a conception of the Deity which represents Him, with Omar Khayyam, as One—

> Whose secret Presence, through Creation's veins
> Running, Quicksilver-like eludes your pains;
>   Taking all forms from Màh to Màhi; and
> They change and perish all—but He remains.

Such a doctrine can only mean that the Divine Substance, under a myriad-fold variety of appearances, is equally diffused through all creation, like the universal ether of science; and such a conception of the Eternal, whatever else it may be, ceases *ipso facto* to be religiously helpful. The counterpart of the theoretical allness would be the practical nothingness of God.[2] But having quite definitely declined to place such a construction upon immanence, we are preserved from the absurdities which flow from it. We may and do hold that all the works of the Lord manifest Him in some manner and in some measure; but, as we already stated in our introductory chapter, not all do so in the same manner or the same measure, and not any of them nor all of them are He. To the specific inquiry, What, if not part of God, is this stone?—we can, indeed, only answer in the words of Tennyson that if we knew what the least object was in itself, we "should know what God and man is." But, dealing with the question more generally, we may say that what inorganic nature shows forth of the indwelling God is His prevailing Power and abiding Law; looking upon the works of Him who "stretcheth out the north over empty space, and hangeth the earth upon nothing," we can but feel that awed admiration of His wisdom and might which is expressed over and over again in the Book of Job. And this impression deepens when we pass upward from the inorganic to the organic creation; for not only do we behold the entire vast spectacle thrilled through and through by one Life, but we are also enabled to discern something of the august Purpose which progressively realises itself in all the phases of the cosmic process. That the God revealed by the universe must transcend the universe in order to be in any real sense its Creator, is self-evident; but that it is His own Energy which pervades it, a present Power operating from within—in other words, that He is immanent in the world, as well as transcendent—is a thought from which we cannot legitimately escape.

When we speak of the immanence of God in nature, therefore, we mean principally immanence of Power; and due weight should be given to this qualification, since its effect is to remove the obstacles we have enumerated above. For it ought to be plain, though in popular discussion it is constantly overlooked, that God cannot be *ethically* present in the unethical, nor *personally* present in the impersonal. And here, it seems to us, we go to the root of our present problem, *viz.*, by re-emphasising what is indispensable to a right conception of this whole doctrine—that immanence is of necessity a matter of degrees. Nature is not moral, and hence does not reveal God's moral character to us; nature is not personal, and therefore, while its operations point with irresistible cogency to personal directivity, does not show forth the Divine Personality as indwelling.

As soon as we grasp this obvious truth, we shall be led to find the answer to that question which, as we saw, presents a stumbling-block to many minds, namely, in what sense it is permissible to affirm the Divine immanence in the animal world. How can God be in the denizens of the jungle, we ask, feeling that to make such an statement concerning Him is to empty the idea of God of all its meaning. Natural, however, as such reasoning is, reflection will show it to be faulty. To use a simple, if necessarily imperfect, illustration, something of man's own being is in all his organs, but not all that makes him man is in every one of them; certainly, his higher faculties are not displayed in the organs designed to fulfil the lower functions of the organism. To proceed to the obvious application— animals are not moral beings, but act, with the occasional exception of such of their number as have been humanised by contact with men, from instinct and not from conscious choice; and for that reason we are not called upon to reconcile the loving-kindness and tender mercy of God with the habits and general behaviour of the lower creation. In ascribing all sorts of moral qualities to animals we simply exhibit the same tendency which leads children to endow lifeless objects both with life and purposiveness. Moral attributes, however, whether good or bad, presuppose conscious choice, a faculty of weighing and if necessary repelling motives; and with such a faculty we have no reason for crediting animals. No doubt, our incurable habit of reading the facts of our own moral nature into the actions of beasts and birds accounts for the vogue alike of Aesop's Fables and of such works as the *Jungle Books*; but what strikes us as cruelty in the tiger is not a moral quality at all, any more than it is a motive of heroism that impels the mongoose to fight cobras. The tiger and the cobra are no more deliberately "cruel" than they could be conceived as deliberately "benevolent"; they are below the ethical level, expressing no character at all, and least of all the character of God.

But if God is immanent in the cosmos as its pervading and sustaining Power and Life; if He is immanent in man as that moral and spiritual principle which reaches out after fuller communion with the Most High: where shall we say that He Himself is *personally present*, since He is not so present either in nature or in man? And assuming that such a supreme and full revelation of God has been given in history, shall we not do well to distinguish in some manner between it and every lesser manifestation of immanence? Mr. W. L. Walker has admirably pointed out that while God is personally present *to* everything, and entirely absent from nothing, yet it is certainly false to imagine that He is "personally inside of everything." "Nothing can happen wholly apart from Him—He is in some measure in everything and being"; but where shall He Himself be found, where shall we look for His very fulness? "He cannot," says Mr. Walker—and we shall not attempt to better his words—"be personally present in anything, or in any being, till there is a being present in the world capable of containing and expressing Him in His essential truth; and that we do not have till we come to Jesus Christ."

And thus we may perhaps claim to have shown, however briefly, in what direction we must look for the solution of our problem of universal immanence—a problem unnecessarily complicated by a plausible but false construction of that doctrine. We conclude that every portion of the cosmos, including our conscious selves, manifests so much, and such aspects, of God as it has the capacity to manifest—His Power, His Purpose, His moral Law, which vindicates its sanctity upon whosoever would violate it; but His own Essence, His Character, could be revealed only in One whose soul harboured no single element at variance with the Divine Goodness, One who could be described as "God manifest in the flesh"—even that unique Son whose oneness with the Father was undimmed and unbroken by any diversity of will. It required the perfect Instrument to give forth the perfect Harmony.

And here a final but important point arises. If the Incarnation of God in Christ is in one sense the highest example of Divine immanence—just as man represents the highest form of animal life—yet in another sense it transcends mere immanence just as truly as humanity transcends the animal creation. We leave this as a suggestion which the reader may develop for himself. So much is certain, that in Christ alone does the edifice of faith reach its culminating point—in Him our questionings receive their complete and final answer, because what we see in Him is not a stray hint or broken gleam, but the pure and quenchless light of God's own Presence. *"No man hath seen God at any time; the only begotten Son, which is in the bosom of the Father, He hath declared Him."*

[1] The Rev. R. J. Campbell, M.A., in a paper on *Divine Immanence and Pantheism*. For the phrase and the Idea of the "allness of God" see also *Rudimental Divine (i.e. Christian) Science*, by Mary Baker Eddy, p. 10.

[2] We cannot forbear quoting two pungent lines of Mr. Hamish Hendry's, in which the outcome of such theosophising seems to be not altogether unjustly described as—

A kind o' thowless Great First Cause, Skinklin' thro' vapour.

CHAPTER II
PANTHEISM: THE SUICIDE OF RELIGION

In speaking of Deism, the theory which explicitly denies the Divine immanence, we already had occasion to acknowledge that quality of intelligibleness which makes this doctrine easy of assimilation, and accounts, *e.g.*, for the success of Islam, the deistic religion *par excellence*, as a propagandist creed. There is, however, another aspect of Deism, none the less real because it is not always recognised at first sight, which perhaps an illustration will serve to bring home to us. We all know what is likely to happen to an estate in the owner's prolonged or permanent absence—it deteriorates; his active interest and personal supervision are wanting, and the results are visible everywhere. Sloth and mismanagement, which his presence would check, go uncorrected, the daily duties are indifferently performed or remain undone, and soon the property as a whole bears unmistakeable traces of neglect. There is always the possibility of the master's return some day, when he will exact an account from his servants; but the long interval which has elapsed since such a visit took place has deprived that mere possibility of any wholesome terror which it might inspire, so that matters drift steadily from bad to worse.

Now, from the deistic point of view, the world may not unfairly be compared to such an estate. God is remote—He may look down upon the terrestrial scene from His far-off heaven, but He does not actively interfere, except by an occasional miracle, which is not the same as direct hour-by-hour superintendence: is it any wonder that the ground should bring forth weeds and brambles rather than flowers and fruit? Is it a wonder that this God-less world should be a dismal place and full of misery, and that human nature, left to itself, should have "no health" in it? It would be matter for wonder if it were otherwise; and thus Deism is well in accord with those gloomier forms of religious thought which for a long time were the generally predominating ones.

The distance between this conception and that which flows from the doctrine of Divine immanence can hardly be measured; it certainly cannot be bridged. The soul to which, through whatever experience, there has come the revelation that God is closer to us than breathing, and nearer than hands or feet, looks out upon a new heaven and a new earth. Once it is understood that God is really and truly in His universe, that He is not infinitely far and inaccessible but infinitely nigh, an encompassing Presence, a fresh light falls upon nature and human nature alike. Viewed in that light, and from the standpoint of this illuminating truth, "the world's no blot for us, nor blank," but the scene of Divine activity and unceasing revelation; for all nature's forces are seen to be the expression of the Divine Energy, and all nature's laws the manifestation of the Divine Will. If God Himself is the Life that stirs within all life, the Reality underlying all phenomena—if we live and move and have our being in Him, and His Spirit dwelleth within us—the direct outcome of such a belief should be a sacred optimism, an assurance that the cosmos "means intensely, and means good."

There can, we think, be little doubt as to the beneficial effects which have accompanied the re-affirmation of this idea in recent times. It is only too true as yet, in the case of many, that "the past, which still holds its ground in the back chambers of the brain, would persuade us that 'tis a demon-haunted world, where not God but the devil rules; we are not yet persuaded that this is a cheerful, homely, well-meaning universe, whose powers, if strict in their working, are nevertheless beneficent and not diabolic." Against these phantasmal fears the doctrine of God's immanence, rightly understood, offers the best of antidotes, and here lies its unquestionable value. At the same time it has already become apparent to us that the suddenness of the stress laid upon that idea has brought new dangers in its train. The temptation is ever to swing round from one extreme to its opposite; and in the present case not a few have carried—or been carried by—the reaction against the belief in God's remoteness so far as to forget, in contemplating the truth that He is "through all and in all," the complementary and equally necessary truth that He is also God over all. Because something of His Mind and Will is expressed by the universe, they not only, as we saw in the previous chapter, conclude that the universe is identical with Him, but that He is no other than the universe which reveals Him. "All is God, and God is All," they exclaim, adding the doctrine of the Godness of all to that of the allness of God; the universe, in their view, is the one Divine and Eternal Being of which everything, including ourselves, is only a phase or partial manifestation; as it is the Divine life which pulses through us, so it is the Divine consciousness which our consciousness expresses, the Divine nature which acts through ours. Here we are face to face with Pantheism full-grown: let us see what is involved in its assumptions, and why the Christian Church must resolutely refuse to make terms with this teaching.

No one would deny that the pantheistic theory, which identifies God with the universe and ourselves with God, has its fascination and glamour—a fascination which is not ignoble on the face of it. The modern founder of Pantheism, Benedict Spinoza, was a man of pure and saintly character, a gentle recluse from the world, lovable and blameless. Nevertheless, we have no hesitation in avowing our belief that the glamour of Pantheism is utterly deceptive; that those who set foot on this inclined plane will find themselves unable—in direct proportion to their mental integrity—to resist conclusions which mean the practical dissolution of religion, in any intelligible sense of that word; and that in the present transitional state of religious opinion it is particularly necessary that the truth about Pantheism should be clearly stated. The test of a theory is not whether it looks symmetrical and self-consistent in the seclusion of the study, but whether it works. If it fails in actual life, it fails altogether; and the one fatal objection to this particular system is that it does not work. Nothing could be more significant than the admission of so representative an exponent of Pantheism as Mr. Allanson Picton, who tells us that one, if not more, of Spinoza's fundamental conceptions "have increasingly repelled rather than attracted religious people." [1] It is the object of the present chapter to show why this must be the case, wherever the implications of his teaching are understood.

Pantheism declares—it practically begins and ends with the declaration—that the universe is God, and that God is the totality of being. Now, try as we will, such a conception can never take the place of the thought of God as our Father, and that for the simple reason that the universe is not even what we mean by personal. As Schopenhauer shrewdly remarked, "To call the universe 'God' is not to explain it, but merely to burden language with a superfluous synonym for the word 'universe.' Whether one says 'the universe is God' or 'the universe is the universe' makes no difference." It is when people no longer know what to do with a Deity, he continues, that they transfer His part to the universe—"which is, properly speaking, only a decent way of getting rid of Him." [2] A totality of being is not the same as a personal God, but the very contrary. Nor is it any consolation to be told that this totality, though not personal, is "super-personal." Such a super-personal Absolute or Whole, to quote Dr. Ballard's penetrating criticism, "is devoid of just those elements which for human experience constitute personality. To our power of vision it matters nothing whether we say that the ultra-violet rays of the spectrum are super-visible or invisible. The pertinent truth is that they are not visible. So, too, that which is not 'merely' personal is not really personal. If the Absolute of philosophy be the super-personal, it is not, in plain truth, personal at all." [3]

Now, a God who is not what we mean by personal can be of no help to us in our religious life. When a congregation of modern worshippers is appealed to in these terms—"Do not, I beseech you, think of God any more as a personal being like yourself, though immeasurably greater"—they are really being asked to commit spiritual suicide. For we cannot hold communion except with a person; we cannot pray to the universe. We can neither give thanks to the universe, nor supplicate it, nor confess to it, nor intercede with it. But a God to whom we cannot pray, with whom we cannot enter into communion, is for all practical purposes no God at all. The only God with whom we can stand in personal, conscious, spiritual relationship must be one who is not identical with the universe, but One in whom, on the contrary, the universe has its being. It is the transcendent God with whom we have to deal in religion; such a God Pantheism does not acknowledge.

But not only is the universe not personal; this god of Pantheism is not ethical either. This "totality" is neither good nor bad, but made up indifferently of all manner of components, and according to Pantheism all of them—the evil as much as the good—are necessary to the perfection of the whole. Thus the pantheist's god has no moral complexion, and such a god is of no use to us. So far as religion is concerned, he—or it—might just as well be non-existent as non-moral. The only Deity whom we can *worship* is One who stands above the world's confusion, its Moral Governor and Righteous Judge.

But Pantheism identifies not only God with the universe, but ourselves with God. Now if this view is accepted, if there is no real dividing line between man and God, then we can only once more point out that we have no personality either; we are mere fragmentary expressions of God's life, without selfhood or self-determination, no more responsible for our acts than a violin for the tune that is played on it. Mr. Picton, speaking with authority, tells us that "to the true pantheist" man is "but a finite mode of infinite Being"; that human personality is only "seeming" [4] and that, from the pantheistic standpoint, the self must be "content to be nothing." That is to say that the consistent pantheist must be a consistent determinist. Logical Pantheism rules out the possibility of sin against man or God—"for who withstandeth His will," seeing that He is the only real Existence? Let a further quotation make this plain. "What," asks Mr. Picton, "are we to say of bad men, the vile, the base, the liar, the murderer? Are they also in God and of God? . . . *Yes, they are.*" [5] And this amazing conclusion—amazing, though involved in his fundamental outlook—is sought to be defended on the ground that we have "no adequate idea" "of the part played by bad men in the Divine Whole"! In other words, the pantheist god expresses himself in a St. Francis, but he also does so in a King Leopold; he is manifested in General Booth and in Alexander Borgia; Jesus Christ is a phase of his being, and so is Judas Iscariot. A sentimental Pantheism may say that God is that in a hero which nerves him to heroism, and that in a mother which prompts her self-sacrifice for her children, for there is none else. But that is only one-half of the truth; arguing from the same premises, we must also say that God is that in the sinner which succumbs to sin, and in the wrong-doer that which takes pleasure in wrong, for there is none else. Once we rub out the distinction between God and man, we rub out all *moral* distinctions as well. If we are not other than He is, how can we act other than He wills? If we hold that the soul is only "a finite mode of God's infinite attribute of thought," part of "the necessary expression of the infinite attributes of eternal Being," the sense of sin can be no more than an illusion.

Or shall we be told that, whatever a man's theoretical Determinism, in practice he will always be conscious of his freedom? The answer is, Yes, perhaps, provided his moral instincts are sound; but the average mortal, when he has to choose between the hard duty and the easy indulgence, will be sorely tempted to find a reason for yielding in his determinist philosophy. And is a doctrine likely to be true which, the moment it is seriously applied, undermines the very foundation of morality, and of which the best that can be said is that people do not consistently apply it? M. Bourget's *Le Disciple* is not a book for everyone; but in it the distinguished author has drawn an instructive picture of the effect of Determinism as a theory upon a self-indulgent man's practice. As Mr. Baring-Gould aptly says, "Human nature is ever prone to find an excuse for getting the shoulder from under the yoke."

Pantheism, as a matter of fact, whichever way we travel, is ultimately compelled to deny the qualitative distinction between good and evil, declaring both to be equally necessary, and thus arrives once more at its conception of a Deity who, though said to be "perfect"—presumably in some "super-moral" sense—is not good, and hence cannot be a possible object of worship for us. How little the pantheist's God can mean to us will be understood when it is stated that, according to Spinoza, man "cannot strive to have God's love to him." [6] Indeed, how could the universe "love" one of its mere passing phases? Is it a wonder that this cheerless creed has "increasingly repelled rather than attracted religious people" when once they have understood its inwardness? We ask for bread and receive—a nebula; we call for our Father, and are told to content ourselves with a totality of being!

And when Pantheism has thus despoiled us of our religious possessions one by one, so far as this life is concerned, what is its message concerning the future? This, that when we die there is an end even of our seeming self-hood; we are once more immersed in the All, the Whole—like a thimbleful of water drawn from the ocean and poured back into the ocean again. This is what Mr. Picton calls "the peace of absorption in the Infinite"; would it not be simpler to call it annihilation, and have done with it? Dissolve a bronze statue and merge it in a mass of molten metal, and it is gone as a statue; dissolve a soul and merge it in the sum of being, and as a soul it is no more. That is not immortality, but a final blotting out—a fit conclusion from those pantheistic premises which, consistently worked out, mean the end of religion, the end of morality, the end of everything.

Pantheism goes about under a variety of aliases to-day, and therein lies an additional danger; for whatever its assumed name or disguise, its essence is always the same, and its very speciousness calls for all our vigilance and determination to fight it. We must not weary of challenging its root-assumption, or of exposing its insidious tendencies; we must not weary of reiterating the truth that God is not identical with the universe, but to be worshipped as the One who is over all; we must insist that His nearness to us and our likeness to Him are not identity with Him—nay, that it is His otherness from us which makes us capable of seeking and finding Him, of experiencing His love, and loving Him in return. From the inhuman speculations of Pantheism we turn with unspeakable gratitude to the revelation of the personal God in the Person of Jesus Christ His Son, whom having seen, we have beheld the Father, and whose are the words, not of annihilation, but of eternal life.

[1] *Pantheism*, p. 15.

[2] Parerga, vol. ii., pp. 101-102.

[3] *The True God*, p. 118.

[4] *Op. cit.*, p. 15.

[5] *Ibid*, p. 69.

[6] J. Allanson Picton, *Spinoza*, p. 213.

CHAPTER III
THE ETHICS OF MONISM

To say that religious thought is passing to-day through a period of peculiar stress is to utter a commonplace so threadbare that one apologises for repeating it. Even the man in the street—or perhaps we ought to say even the man in the pew, the average member of a Christian Church—is aware that certain potent forces have been for some time past directing a series of sustained assaults upon what were until recently all but unquestioned beliefs; nor, if he is capable of appreciating facts, will he deny—though he may deplore it—that to all seeming these attacks have been attended by a considerable measure of success. If, however, our man in the pew were asked to specify what forces he had in his mind, he would probably in nine cases out of ten point to two such, and two alone, *viz.*, natural science and Biblical criticism, which, he would tell us, had between them created an atmosphere in which the old views of Scriptural authority found it more and more difficult to maintain themselves.

Such an estimate of the situation would be true so far as it went; yet it would omit to take account of a third factor, a solvent far less obvious in its workings, but far more disintegrating in its effects. The factor to which we are referring is philosophy; while science and criticism have overthrown certain traditional ramparts, a type of philosophy has sprung up, slowly undermining the very foundations; or, to vary the simile, while the former two have captured certain outworks, the latter has made its way to within striking distance of the citadel, and that the more unobserved because attention has been focussed almost exclusively upon the more imposing performances of the critic and the biologist.

As a matter of fact, religion never had, nor could have, anything to fear from these two quarters, which—as we can now see—could not in any way touch the essence of religious faith, as distinguished from some of its temporary forms; on the other hand, that very essence might be imperilled by a false but plausible philosophy, and grave practical consequences in the domain of conduct might arise from its spread. For if it is accurate to say that behind every ethic there stands—whether avowed or unavowed—a certain metaphysic, the converse holds true no less; every philosophy, in the exact proportion in which it is *ex animo* accepted, will tend to produce its ethical counterpart. What we submit in all seriousness is that the only real danger to religion that is to be apprehended to-day—a danger to which it is impossible to blind ourselves—is that involved in a certain metaphysical outlook, whose continued growth in popularity cannot but ere long produce its own results in the field of practice.

The philosophy in question is intimately related to that Pantheism at some of whose implications we were glancing in our last chapter; if we refer to it here and subsequently by the name of Monism, under which it has of late obtained a considerable vogue in this country, it must be understood that we do not mean what Dr. Ballard calls _Theo_monism, but a far less carefully thought-out and tested theory of life, which at the present time is making a successful appeal to multitudes of inexact thinkers. The fundamental idea common to this school is that the universe, including our individualities or what we think such, constitutes only one being, and manifests only one will, which all its phenomena express. Separateness of existence, according to such a view—which, after all, represents only the extreme logic of Pantheism—is, of course, a chimaera, and so, *a fortiori*, must separate volition be. The only real will—*i.e.*, the will of the universe—is regarded as good and right; and since there is no other will but that one, and seeing that none resists or inhibits it, it is ever being carried out, continuously operative. To call this will even "prevailing" would be a misuse of language, since there is no other will for it to prevail against.

Now, regarded merely in the abstract, this conception might be treated as a harmless eccentricity or speculative aberration, and is likely to be so treated by the ordinary "practical" man, with his contempt for "theories," and his pathetic conviction that speculation does not matter; let us, however, see what is implied in this particular speculative theory. From the primary assumption of this philosophy it follows with an irresistible cogency that there is no such thing as real, objective evil. Sin, if the term be retained at all, can at most be only a blunder. Evil is only an inexact description of a lesser good, or good in the making. Indeed, properly considered—*i.e.*, from the monistic standpoint—evil is a mere negation, a shadow where light should be; or to be quite logical, evil is that which is not—in other words, there is no evil, except to deluded minds, whose business is to get quit of their delusion. The one and only cosmic will being declared good, it follows that for the monist "all's right with the world," in a sense scarcely contemplated by Browning when he penned that most dubious aphorism. We propose briefly to show how this creed works out—what is its ethical counterpart or issue—not by arguing *in vacuo* what it *must* be, but by presenting to the reader three selected illustrations taken from the writings of as many exponents of this type of Monism.

In his volume *First and Last Things*—a work which he significantly calls "a confession of faith and rule of life"—Mr. H. G. Wells avows himself a believer in the "Being of the Species," and, prospectively at least, in "the eternally conscious Being of all things." The individual as such is merely an "experiment of the species for the species," and without significance *per se*; we are "episodes in an experience greater than ourselves," "incidental experiments in the growing knowledge and consciousness of the race." Mr. Wells's fundamental act of faith is a firm belief in "the ultimate rightness and significance of things," including "the wheel-smashed frog on the road, and the fly drowning in the milk." In other words, all is just as it has to be; regrets, remorses and discontents exist only for the "unbeliever" in this truth, while, speaking for himself, the author frankly says, "I believe . . . that my defects and uglinesses and failures, just as much as my powers and successes, are things that are necessary and important." "In the last resort," he concludes his book, "I do not care whether I am seated on a throne, or drunk, or dying in a gutter. I follow my leading. In the ultimate I know, though I cannot prove my knowledge in any way whatever, that everything is right, and all things mine."

Certainly, this is uncompromising candour; but it is also,—though Mr. Wells, strangely enough, calls himself a believer in freewill—the most uncompromising Determinism conceivable. And this Determinism follows quite inevitably from Mr. Wells's monistic premises—belief in a cosmic "scheme" every part of which is ultimately right. An end in the gutter or on the gallows may be as necessary to that scheme's perfection as a life spent in strenuous goodness. Whatever is, is right. It can be hardly necessary to point out that such a belief, consistently entertained, puts an end to all moral effort; we "follow our leading"—*i.e.*, we do not drive, but drift. Arguing from his own premises, it is absolutely vain for Mr. Wells to wax indignantly eloquent over social abuses, as when he says:—

I see the grimy millions who slave for industrial production; I see some who are extravagant and yet contemptible creatures of luxury, and some leading lives of shame and indignity; . . . I see gamblers, fools, brutes, toilers, martyrs. Their disorder of effort, the spectacle of futility, fills me with a passionate desire to end waste, to create order. (p. 99.)

But why, we ask, should Mr. Wells feel this passionate desire, if all the failures and uglinesses of life are "necessary and important"? How, on this assumption, are existing social ills to be remedied—nay, why *should* they be remedied, why should they be stigmatised as ills, seeing that "everything is right"? Let Mr. Wells once take his principles seriously enough to apply them, and personal as well as social reform is at an end. Perhaps it may be permissible to say that of all forms of Determinism the most irrational is that optimistic form which deprecates discontent with things as they are as a mark of "unbelief."

Mr. Wells, however, while his influence is a very considerable one, utters his teaching from outside the Christian Church, and very properly disavows the

Christian name; what must give us pause is to find the monistic ethics being preached and taught by official exponents of the Christian religion. What, *e.g.*, can we think of a statement like the following, which we quote from the columns of a religious journal?

There are people who think it is an evidence of superior Culture to show themselves pained by certain things; but it is not really that; they are pained because they are not cultured enough, or in the right way...

> Nothing is good or ill
> But thinking makes it so.

They think it desirable to dislike things because they dislike them; if they thought it desirable not to dislike them, they would not dislike them.

Again, no one will accuse this writer of want of frankness; according to him, there is simply no such thing as objective evil—acts and individuals have no moral qualities or characters, but are such as we think them, and our business is so to think of them that they will not pain us. If we only knew aright, we should not regard anything as bad. If we are pained by the thought of fifty thousand hungry children in London elementary schools, or by the condition of Regent Street at night, it is because we are not "cultured" enough—we have not the right *gnosis*. When we reflect that anyone who consistently believes that "nothing is good or ill, but thinking makes it so," will inevitably, first or last, apply that comforting maxim to his own acts, we can see in what direction the ethics of Monism—in reality a return to the ultra-subjectivism of the Sophists, who made man the measure of all things—are likely to lead men. And yet, if the monistic presuppositions are valid—if the universe in all its phases expresses only one will—we do not see how these conclusions can be repelled.

But it is, perhaps, our last illustration, drawn from yet another writer of the same school, which will exhibit both the teaching under discussion and its practical dangers in the clearest light. We are told that—

There is no will that is not God's will. I do not mean that yours is not real, or that any man's is not real, but I do mean that nothing can happen to any of God's children—no matter how evil the intention of the person who does it, or how seemingly meaningless the calamity that causes it—which is not in some way the sacrament of God's love to us, and His call upon our highest energies. In a true and real sense, therefore, it is God's own doing and meant for our greater glory; ... I believe in the infinitude of wisdom and love; *there is nothing else.*

Those who will take the moderate trouble of translating these words from the abstract into the concrete will need no further demonstration of the moral implications of this type of Monism. "There is no will"—not even the most brutalised or the most debauched—"that is not God's will." "Nothing can happen to any of God's children"—say, to the natives of the Congo or to a Jewish community during a Russian *pogrom*—but is God's call upon their highest energies: wherefore they ought, assuredly, to be thankful to King Leopold's emissaries and the Tsar's faithful Black Hundreds! But let us apply this thesis to yet another case, which will bring out its full character: if an English girl—one of God's children—is snared away by a ruffian, under pretext of honest employment, to some Continental hell, then we are to understand that the physical and moral ruin which awaits the victim is "in some way the sacrament of God's love" to her—"in a true and real sense it is God's own doing," and meant for her greater glory! We have no hesitation in saying that such teaching strikes us as fraught with infinite possibilities of moral harm, the more so because of the rather mawkish sentimentality with which it is decked out; for if any scoundrel is really the instrument of God's will, why should he be blamed for his scoundrelism? And we observe how yet once more, by a glib and vapid phrase—"I believe in the infinitude of wisdom and love; *there is nothing else*"—the fact of evil has been triumphantly got rid of. In words, that is to say, but not in reality; for in reality there is a great deal else—sin, and shame, and remorse, and heartbreak, and despair; against the first of which we need to be warned, in order that we may escape the rest.

We are quite prepared to be told that our anxieties are groundless, because "no one will ever draw such inferences as these." To this we reply, firstly, that these are the logical and legitimate inferences from the principles enunciated; and secondly, that we do not at all share the particular kind of optimism which trusts that good luck will prevent the application of these theories to practical life. We are living in an age of wide-spread intellectual unsettlement, an age presenting the difficult problem of a vast half-educated public, ready to fall an easy prey to all manner of specious sophistries, especially when they are dressed up in the garb of a pseudo-mysticism; we must above all remember that human nature is habitually prone to welcome whatever will serve as an excuse for throwing off the irksome restraints of moral discipline. That is why we repeat that the one real danger religion has to face to-day is the danger arising from the spread of a false philosophy, whose tenets are ultimately incompatible with Christian morals. The worst heresies are moral heresies; and of the views we have been discussing we say roundly that their falseness is sufficiently proved by their ethical implications. "A good tree cannot bring forth evil fruit; therefore by their fruits ye shall know them." Against all the insidious attempts that are made to-day to minimise or explain away moral evil—

attempts with which we shall deal in greater detail at a later stage—we have to reaffirm the reality and exceeding sinfulness of sin; more particularly, in combating the preposterous notion of man's oneness with God as something already realised, we have to insist with renewed emphasis that salvation, so far from being self-understood, is a prize only to be won by a hard struggle, nor shut the door upon the dread possibility of that prize being missed. There are perhaps few truths to which it is more desirable that we should pay renewed attention than that expressed in the saying, "*When belief waxes unsound, practice becomes uncertain.*" Certainly, the ethics of Monism supply a case in point.

CHAPTER IV
MONISM AND THE INDIVIDUAL

When Tennyson, in *Locksley Hall*, wrote the line declaring that "the individual withers and the world is more and more," he might have been inditing a prophecy summing up those modern tendencies which have engaged our attention in preceding chapters. And there are perhaps few more important questions before us to-day than this—whether Tennyson's prophecy is to be fulfilled, whether the individual is to be allowed to "wither," and the world to become more and more. There are those who hold that such a consummation is devoutly to be wished; there are those who regard any movement making in such a direction with something more than suspicion.

Let us say at once that in discussing the status of the individual, we are not referring—at least, not directly—to the struggle between Individualism and Socialism. We know that individualists express the fear that under a socialist *régime* there would be an end to individual initiative, while socialists retort that the chief sin of the competitive system is that it crushes and destroys individuality; but between the contentions of these rival schools of economics we are not attempting to adjudicate. Perhaps we cannot better indicate the scope of our subject than by quoting from two recent theological works, written from such widely differing points of view as Professor Peake's *Christianity: Its Nature and its Truth*, and Professor Bousset's *The Faith of a Modern Protestant*:—

"It is only in it"—*viz.*, in Christianity—says the learned Primitive Methodist theologian, "that the individual has received his true place. In antiquity the worth of the individual was greatly under-estimated; he was unduly subordinated to the community. But the Christian religion, by insisting on the infinite value of each human soul, and by asserting the greatness of its destiny, supplied an immense incentive to the attainment by each of the highest within reach. The doctrine of the worth of man is, to all who accept it, a powerful stimulus in the struggle to a fuller and deeper life. An interest in mankind in the mass is compatible with heartless indifference to the lot of individuals" (p. 88).

"The Gospel," declares the Göttingen modernist, "announces a God who seeks and desires above all else the individual human soul. It unites, in a security and closeness hitherto unknown, belief in God with the importance of the individual human life. It is the religion of religious individualism raised to its highest point." (p. 36).

Such concurrence of testimony from two such different quarters is as remarkable as it is significant; and this brings us to our point. The question with which we are confronted to-day, and which our civilisation must either answer aright or perish, is not whether an individualist or a socialist state would be more conducive to the individual's self-realisation, but whether Christianity is right or wrong in its doctrine of the individual's paramount importance. The issue, as we shall try to show, lies between Christianity on the one hand and Monism on the other. From the Christian point of view the individual matters supremely; from that of Monism the beginning of wisdom is that the individual should recognise and acquiesce in his utter insignificance.

As in our last chapter we glanced at the monistic ethics, so in the present one we propose to inquire briefly first into the social and then into the religious implications of this theory, which it must be remembered is receiving a good deal of support, and meeting with a large measure of acceptance just now. Turning, then, to the social side first of all, no one, of course, would say that Socialism as such was monistic; on the other hand it is easy to understand the attraction of Socialism for those whose philosophy is Monism. They will embrace the economic teachings of Collectivism the more eagerly in exact proportion to their root-conviction that the only thing that matters is the totality of things, while the individual, *per se*, does not count at all. That is the conception which underlies the Socialism of a writer like Mr. Wells, who is in nothing more emphatic than in asserting that the individual as such has no value at all. "Our individualities," he says, "are but bubbles and clusters of foam upon the great stream of the blood of the species." "The race is the drama, and we are the incidents." "In so far as we are individuals . . . we are accidental, disconnected, without significance." And when we ask for what we should strive and labour, if not for the good of individual men and women, his answer is that we ought to work for the Species, for the Race, for what he calls a great physical and mental being, to wit, Mankind.

Now we believe that this philosophy, consistently embraced, is utterly devoid of the dynamic which can generate any great social reform. The smallest and forlornest actual slum baby appeals to our sympathy immeasurably more than a vast, dim aggregate of indistinguishable items called the Race; for we have actually met the slum-baby, and we have never met—what is more, we shall never meet—the Race. This tendency to treat the individual as negligible is as futile as it is inhuman; in the long run it will be found that he who loveth not his brother whom he hath seen, cannot love the Race which he hath not seen. No matter by how many times we multiply nothing, the result is still—nothing. If the individuals do not count, neither can the species which is made up of such individuals. Or, if "the Race is the drama, and we are the incidents," it must be observed that no great and noble drama can be strung together out of trivial and unmeaning incidents. All the talk about Mankind as the greater being, "the great and growing Being of the Species," "the eternally conscious Being of all things," is only the old, thin, unsatisfying idolatry of Positivism. If we wish to be social reformers in earnest we must take care of the individuals, and the race will take care of itself.

That the monistic denial of all individual significance should lead to the denial of a future life is only what we should expect; for if man, as such, does not *matter*, why should he *survive*? On the other hand, the more we care for the individual, refusing to regard him merely as "an experiment of the species for the species," the more irresistibly shall we be impelled to believe that this life is not all. It is the inestimable achievement of Christianity, by its insistence on the infinite value of the soul, to have given the strongest impetus and support to belief in personal immortality. That, however, is an aspect of our subject which demands, and will subsequently come up for, separate treatment.

What, for the present, we must yet once more point out, as we did in the preceding chapter, is this—that wide as is the influence of a non-Christian writer like Mr. Wells, the danger of such teaching is intensified when it is given by those who profess Christianity. Doubtless, Bousset is right when he points to the closer contact between East and West as one of the causes of the growth in our midst of a type of religion in which "the human ego is put on one side and almost reduced to zero." Doubtless, also, he is correct in saying "the adherents of this kind of religion will be chiefly found in circles where people do not regard religion seriously, where they desire and accept religion as aesthetic enjoyment." Nevertheless, the evil attending this type of teaching is, to our thinking, great and serious, designed to undermine selfhood and to set up a species of dry-rot at the very centre.

Let us again show what we mean by quoting from an actual utterance: "God," we read, "is supposed to be thinking more about us than about anything else—a rather arrogant assumption when we come to think of it, considering what specks of dust we are amid these myriads of stars and suns whirling through space like motes in a ray of light—and the great object of His solicitude is to get us individually to toe the mark of Christ-likeness." If this view be the true one, the writer went on to ask, why do questions like unemployment, the Budget, the uprising of nationalism in Turkey, etc., bulk so largely in our thought? These topics, he says, have "little or no relation to the question of saving the individual soul, as commonly understood." How, he demands, does the actual life of every day fit into "that view of the scheme of things which bids us believe that the silent God above us is principally anxious about just one thing, the moral recovery and ingathering of these individual souls one by one"? The answer is given with characteristic confidence: "It does not fit into it at all; *if God be as anxious about that as we are assured He is, He has a queer way of showing it.*"

Here we have a conception of man and his place in the sum of things fundamentally at one with that of Mr. Wells, and as utterly irreconcilable with that of Christianity. Not only does the individual not matter in himself; he does not even matter to God. The idea of the soul's infinite value to God is held up to derision, and so is the idea of God's interest in individual character; man, the atom, must not think that the Creator is specially anxious for his fate, and is bidden to measure his insignificance against the vastness of the heavenly bodies; and in conclusion we are pertly told that if God really cares about the individual as such, "He has a queer way of showing it." In this view—the view of Monism—it is indeed true that "the individual withers, and the world is more and more."

We say that the issue is plain; it lies between Monism and Christianity; if the one is true, the other must be rejected. On which side shall we cast our verdict? For a warning example we have only to glance at the case of Buddhism, in which, the value of human individuality having been steadily lowered, "the other main factor is religion, belief in God, was likewise lost" (Bousset). But, turning to a more detailed examination of the statement just quoted, it is hardly necessary to discuss the astounding suggestion that man must not take himself too seriously by the side of the immensities of suns and stars. Such a view merely betrays a spiritual perception miles below that of the Psalmist, who saw man, to all appearance a negligible speck, yet in reality made by the Almighty little lower than the angels, and crowned with glory and honour. Neither need we combat at length the strangely superficial notion that such questions as unemployment, the Budget, etc., have little or no relation to that of saving the individual soul, as commonly understood. If they have no relation to *that* subject, they are hardly worth considering; but the fact is that the regulation of industry, the distribution of wealth—these and all other questions derive their importance solely from the manner in which they affect individual men, women and children, fitting or unfitting them for the life that now is and that which is to come. A good deal might be said of the temper which makes fun of the idea of God's "solicitude to get us individually to toe the mark of Christ-likeness"; but we may leave that unhappy phrase to be its own comment.

The attitude of Christianity to our question is perfectly clear. Christianity, in teaching each frailest, poorest human unit to address God as Father, affirms in unmistakeable accents the Eternal's personal interest in and care for the individual soul, and by so doing ennobles every human life that falls under the sway of the Gospel. It is Christianity's master-thought that to the Father from whom all fatherhood is named each one of His children is personally dear, and that His desire is for the salvation of each one. To the cheap and ugly sneer that God has a "queer way" of manifesting His concern for us as individuals, the Christian consciousness has its own answer; how, in any case, such a sneer could come from the same source from which we previously quoted the statement that "nothing can happen to any of God's children which is not in some way the sacrament of God's love to us," we do not profess to understand. We are not mere individual organ-stops, each without use or significance apart from the rest, waiting for our mutual dissonances to be swallowed up in some "music of the whole," but members of a family, each with a place in the Parent's heart and thought. Finally, to the Christian there is one last, crowning proof of the soul's value for God, and God's yearning for the soul; that proof is Calvary. To the Christian there is one experience which settles this problem fully and finally for him; it is the experience which Paul embodied in the cry, "He loved me, and gave Himself for me."

For Monism the individual is a mere surface ripple on an infinite ocean, alike impermanent and impersonal; for Christianity the soul is a child of the Father of all souls, loved with an everlasting love. Between these two conceptions we have to choose, remembering that each utterly excludes the other. There is no third alternative.

CHAPTER V
THE DIVINE PERSONALITY

While in our last three chapters we have been dealing with certain theories which implicitly or explicitly deny the Divine Personality, and while an impersonal God can be, as we have already seen, of no value for religion, there is no mistaking the fact that this very question—whether, *i.e.*, it is possible and legitimate for us to think of God as personal—constitutes one of the most typical of modern "difficulties." It is probably correct to say that this difficulty, like others we have reviewed, dates practically from the collapse of Deism, a creed which possessed a certain hard lucidity satisfying to many for the very reason that it required no very profound insight for its understanding. That a Deity localised in a far-away heaven, seated on a celestial throne and surrounded by an angelic court, should be a person, like any other sovereign, presented no problem to the understanding; but if God was not merely transcendent but also immanent—not merely somewhere but in some indefinable manner everywhere—then to predicate personality of such a One seemed a very paradox. In one of Feuillet's novels there occurs a phrase which sums up in a few expressive words a very common spiritual misadventure: the hero says, "*J'avais vu disparaître parmi les nuages la tête de ce bon vieillard qu'on appelle Dieu*"—"I had seen the head of that good old man called God disappear amongst the clouds." His naïve material conception of the Eternal had dissolved—and dissolved into nothingness. May we not surmise that nine times out of ten this is precisely what has happened when we hear the question asked, "But how *can* God be personal?"

In by far the greater number of cases, that is to say, the problem arises simply and solely from the questioner's failure to dissociate *personality* from *materiality*; a "person" suggests to him a tangible, visible, ponderable form, with arms and legs and organs of sense—and when he has reflected sufficiently to understand that such a description cannot apply to God, he concludes that *therefore* God cannot be personal. The next step is usually that, having seen this visibly outlined Deity disappear *parmi les nuages*, he passes into absolute unbelief; for somehow an impersonal "Power," while it may possibly inspire awe, cannot move us to worship, cannot present to us a moral imperative, cannot, above all, either claim our love or give us its affection. It is really the identical difficulty, stated a little more pretentiously, which the "rationalist" author of *The Churches and Modern Thought* presents to us by remarking that in all our experience that which makes up personality is "connected with nerve structures," so that we cannot attribute such a quality to "a Being who is described to us as devoid of any nerve structure." "I know of no answer," he quaintly adds, "that could be called satisfactory from a theistic standpoint." [1] It is evident that Mr. Vivian does not remember the famous passage in the *Essay on Theism* where John Stuart Mill explains that "the relation of thought to a material brain is no metaphysical necessity, but simply a constant co-existence within the limits of observation," and concludes that although "experience furnishes us with no example of any series of states of consciousness" without an accompanying brain, "it is as easy to imagine such a series of states without as with this accompaniment." [2] According to Mill—hardly a champion of orthodoxy—there is no reason in the nature of things why "thoughts, emotions, volitions and even sensations" should be necessarily dependent upon or connected with "nerve structures "; so that Mr. Vivian's argument palpably fails.

But what about this popular notion which identifies personality with materiality, and therefore denies the former attribute to God? One would think that even the most circumscribed experience, or reflection on such experience, must suffice to dispose of such a misapprehension; let us use the most obvious of illustrations for showing where the error lies. We have only to imagine one of those everyday tragedies that make a short newspaper paragraph—say, the case of a man passing a house in process of erection, and being killed on the spot by a piece of falling timber. He is left as a material form; he is decidedly not left as a person. Something has disappeared in that fatal moment that no one had ever seen or handled— his self-consciousness, his intelligence, his will, his affections, his moral sense: *with* these he was a person; *without* them, he is a corpse. If, then, it is these unseen, intangible qualities, and not flesh and bones, muscle and "nerve structure," that constitute *human* personality, is it not rather childish to argue that, unless God possesses a body of some sort, the *Divine* Personality is a contradiction in terms? If we can validly affirm in the Deity qualities corresponding to those which in human beings we call consciousness, intelligence, etc., we shall obviously be compelled to assign personality to Him; the question is, Have we sufficient grounds for making such an affirmation?

But before we are allowed to answer that question, we have to meet another preliminary objection; for it seems that we are in conflict with philosophy—or, to be more exact, with a certain philosophy which, while no longer perhaps in the heyday of its influence with students, still enjoys a good deal of popular vogue. We are, of course, referring to the Spencerian system, in which the word "Absolute" is used as a synonym for what we should call the Deity; but, argues the Spencerian, since "Absolute is that which exists out of all relation," [3] whereas "even intelligence or consciousness itself is conceivable only as a relation," it follows that "the Absolute cannot be thought of as conscious." But if God cannot even be thought of as conscious, how much less can He be thought of as personal!

Such an inference would, indeed, be irresistible if only the premises on which it rests were sound. But is it legitimate, we ask, to identify God with "the Absolute," or is not this merely a way of begging the question? "Absolute is that which exists out of all relation," we were just told, and such a genuine Absolute would be genuinely "unknowable," because its very existence could not be so much as guessed at; but the Spencerian Absolute is the most certain of certainties, described by Professor Hudson as "the one Eternal Reality, the corner-stone of all our knowledge"— otherwise as "the Infinite and Eternal Energy from which all things proceed." But the corner-stone of all our knowledge can be such only because, so far from being unknowable, it is intimately related to all our experience—which is tantamount to saying that it is not absolute at all; and again, if God be the Infinite and Eternal Energy from which all things proceed, that Energy must be thought of as related to all things—in other words, it is the very reverse of absolute. And hence the imaginary impossibility of thinking of the Deity as conscious and intelligent vanishes at one stroke. If God were really absolute, in the sense of the definition quoted above, it would certainly be, as Professor Hudson says, "from the standpoint of philosophical exactness" quite inadmissible "to speak of the Divine Will, or a Personal Creator, or an intelligent Governor of the universe"; but as we have seen that this absoluteness is purely fictitious, it follows that we may legitimately inquire whether consciousness, intelligence, will—and hence personality—are predicable of God, without heeding a veto which rests on imaginary foundations.

It is true Professor Hudson raises two further objections; these, however, will not long detain us. We are informed in the first place that "the further progress of thought 'must force men hereafter to drop the higher anthropomorphic characters given to the First Cause, as they have long since dropped the lower'"; but since our guide, a few pages later, quotes with approval the dictum that "unless we cease to think altogether, we *must* think anthropomorphically," we may be pardoned for declining to believe that "the further progress of thought must force men hereafter" to "cease to think altogether." Such a suicide of thought would furnish an odd comment upon philosophic "progress." We shall, of course, continue to think anthropomorphically of God; our thought will thus inevitably fall short of the Reality, but it will be truer than if we did not think of Him at all. Again, Divine Personality is declared to be a self-contradiction because

"Personality implies limitation, or it means nothing at all. To talk of an Infinite Person, therefore, is to talk of something that is at once infinite and finite, unconditioned and conditioned, unlimited and limited—an impossibility."

To this plea there are, however, two answers. The first may be made in the unprejudiced words of Mr. Vivian, who observes,[4]

"We must not forget that in philosophy and theology the word 'person' simply implies 'a nature endowed with consciousness,' and does not involve limits."

But secondly, without committing ourselves to Professor Hudson's dictum that personality implies limitation, we have to point out that we are not concerned to defend any inference that might be drawn from the infinity, in the sense of the "allness" of God. We do not deny, but on the contrary affirm, that in the act of creation God imposes limitations upon Himself; so that this last obstacle also is disposed of.

So far, then, we have dealt with the *a priori* arguments against the Personality of God, and have seen why none of these—neither that from His non-materiality, nor from His alleged absoluteness or infinity—raises any real bar to His being thought of as personal. We are now in a position to inquire positively whether there is sufficient ground for regarding Him as conscious, intelligent and purposive; if He possesses these qualities, we repeat that He certainly possesses that of personality.

The method by which we must proceed is obvious, and will at once occur to the reader who recalls our opening chapter; the question resolves itself simply into this—Are the phenomena of nature such as to indicate intelligence and directivity in their Cause? We submit that incontrovertible proof of the *absence* of such directive intelligence would be furnished, if the world were, as a matter of fact, chaotic—if it disclosed neither regularity nor continuity—if, in a word, we could never be sure what would happen next. True, in such a state of things life itself could not be sustained, for life is only possible in a world of orderly sequences and uniform laws; but seeing that as a matter of fact such orderly sequences and uniform laws meet us everywhere in nature, is not the inference fairly inevitable? Let us be quite clear on one point: there are two ways, and two only, in which any phenomenon can be accounted for—design or chance; what is not purposed must be accidental. Does, then, nature impress us as the outcome of chance? If we saw a faultlessly executed mathematical diagram illustrating a proposition in Euclid, should we really be satisfied with the statement that it represented the random pencil-strokes made by a blindfolded child ignorant of geometry? On the other hand, if a fretful baby is allowed to divert himself by hammering the piano keys, is the result ever remotely akin to a tune? We know perfectly well that we never get harmony, order, beauty, rationality by accident; and there is only one other alternative—design, purpose, guidance. Professor Fiske quotes a quaint observation of Kepler's illustrating this very point, which we may be allowed to reproduce:—

Yesterday, when weary with writing and my mind quite dusty with considering these atoms, I was called to supper, and a salad was set before me. "It seems then," said I aloud, "that if pewter dishes, leaves of lettuce, grains of salt, drops of oil and vinegar, and slices of eggs, had been floating about in the air from all eternity, it might at last happen by chance that there would come a salad." "Yes," says my wife, "but not so nice and well-dressed as mine is!"

Mrs. Kepler's shrewd, homely remark gives its last touch of absurdity to the suggestion that a world which we see to be pervaded by unfailing law has come together by sheer, incalculable accident. Not so much as a salad of respectable calibre could be accounted for upon such a theory; how much less credible is it that the universe began with a cosmic dance of unconscious atoms whirled along by unconscious forces, and happening so to combine as to produce order and sequence, life and consciousness, will and affection!

But not only does the universe exhibit a sublime order which is the very contrary of what we can associate with the blind workings of chance; not only do the circling immensities of the stars and the microscopic perfections of the snow-crystals alike point to a shaping and directing Mind and Will: what nature reveals—what is implied in the very term evolution—is not merely order but progress. As Fiske has it, "Whatever else may be true, the conviction is brought home to us that in all this endless multifariousness there is one single principle at work, that *all is tending towards an end that was involved in the very beginning.*" In other words, the supreme certainty brought home to us by the researches of modern science is that all creation is thrilled through by an all-encompassing Purpose. We really ask for no more than such an admission; that, in short, is our case. We can clinch the whole argument with one quiet sentence of Mr. Chesterton's: "Where there is a purpose, there is a person." If Mr. Spencer's "Infinite and Eternal Energy, from which all things proceed" is purposive, that is equivalent to saying that God is what we mean by personal.

But ought we not to have shown first of all that He is conscious? No, for the greater includes the less, and purpose is unthinkable apart from consciousness. In saying this we are aware that a philosopher like Eduard von Hartmann speaks of "the wisdom of the Unconscious," of "the mechanical devices which It employs," of "the direction of the goal intended by the Unconscious," etc., etc.; but this, we are bound to say, is to empty words of their meaning. To intend, to direct anything requires at least that the one so doing should be conscious of what it is he is doing. And consciousness, intelligence, directivity are constituents never found apart from personality. But, we are told, "the choice lies, not between personality and something lower, but between personality and something inconceivably higher." [5] We reply that we have already made the acquaintance of this idea of a "super-personal" Deity, and found that for all practical—*i.e.*, religious—purposes the super-personal is simply the impersonal under another name.[6] And when we remember that the "inconceivably higher than personal" ultimate Reality of the agnostic possesses neither consciousness, nor will, nor intelligence, we simply fail to see how a Power lacking these attributes could be even personal, to say nothing of its being *more* than personal. Be this, however, as it may, the decisive fact remains that we are persons, and therefore personality is the highest category under which we can think; and if we, the children of the Eternal, are endowed with personality, it is sufficient for us to know that a cause must be at least adequate to produce the effects that have flowed from it. Nothing can be evolved but what was first involved. On this ground alone, whatever else God may be, He is at least personal; and that is all we were anxious to establish.

That is all—but it is also all-important; for it cannot be too emphatically insisted that without a personal God religion simply ceases to be. It is a strange and delusive fancy on Professor Hudson's part, and that of a good many people, that "the religious emotions" will survive the de-ethicising, depersonalising of the Deity, and that men will remain "deeply religious" even when it is recognised that the "Great Enigma," the "eternal and inscrutable energy," the "ultimate Reality" cannot be spoken of as "a Personal Creator, or an intelligent Governor of the universe." For our own part, we find it difficult to believe that such a forecast could have been framed by anyone possessing a first-hand knowledge of what "the religious emotions" are; we say with the utmost confidence that no such emotions can be felt towards a Power which "cannot be thought of as conscious," let alone as benevolent or personally interested in us. We well know that we can be nothing to such a Power—nor can It be anything to us; for a God who does not care, does not count. We cannot commune with this chill and awesome Unknown; we can only pray to One who hears; we can only love One who has first loved us. In the last analysis, an "impersonal Deity" such as one hears occasionally spoken of, is a mere contradiction in terms, the coinage of confused and inaccurate thought. Where the meaning of personality is so much as understood, doubt as to the Divine Personality vanishes; and least of all will that truth be doubted by those who see the supreme revelation of God in Jesus Christ. He, the Incarnate Son, has shown us, not a Power but a Person—the Person of the Father—and, today as of old, "it sufficeth us."

[1] *The Churches and Modern Thought*, by Philip Vivian, p. 231.

[2] *Three Essays on Religion*, R.P.A. reprint, p. 85.

[3] This and subsequent quotations are taken from pp. 108-119 of Prof. Hudson's *Introduction to the Philosophy of Herbert Spencer*.

[4] Op. cit., p. 231.

[5] Hudson, *op. cit.*, p. 116.

[6] *Supra*, p. 46.

CHAPTER VI

EVIL *versus* DIVINE GOODNESS

That the renewed emphasis upon the Divine immanence must have for one of its effects that of raising the problem of evil afresh, and in a particularly acute form, will be obvious to anyone who has thought out for himself the implications of that doctrine. Dark and pressing enough before, this particular problem has, in appearance at least, been both complicated and accentuated by the displacement of Deism. If, as we have argued on a previous occasion, there is a certain causal connection between Deism and a somewhat sombre outlook upon the world, on the other hand the existence of evil seemed to fit in better with a view of God which represented Him as outside the universe than with one which insists upon His indwelling in creation. If the earth was the scene and playground of undivine agencies which work their will while the Divine control is withdrawn, then many things became comparatively easy of comprehension; indeed, there was a certain consolation in the thought that—

> All the things that had been so wrong
> After all would not last for long,

but that ultimately God would resume the supreme control He had temporarily abandoned, while the Power of darkness would be bound and cast into the abyss. If, however, we must think of Him as omnipresent and for that reason directly and uninterruptedly cognisant of all, then the plain man can only ask himself with a deepening wonder why an all-good and unimaginably powerful Being should permit evils of every description to lay waste His own creation. "No one can enter into the house of the strong, and spoil his goods, except he first bind the strong"; and since a direct overpowering of God by Satan is out of the question, is not the assumption to which we are driven this—that the Strong One is absent while His goods are being spoiled, and that it is this very absence of which the spoiler has taken advantage? Somehow, we feel, if He were really present—as present as the doctrine of immanence would have us believe—He would actively assert Himself against wrongs and abuses; and when we think of the blood and tears that are shed the world over as the result of disordered desire, industrial greed and political misrule, we find it difficult not to echo the words of psalmist and prophet, "Why standest Thou afar off, O Lord? Why hidest Thou Thyself in times of trouble?" "Verily Thou art a God that hidest Thyself."

In saying this we do not suggest that such an attempt to explain the phenomena of evil by God's supposed absence from the world is defensible; we do say that the belief in His all-encompassing nearness makes those phenomena even more difficult of explanation than they were before. The devout deist could always comfort himself with the thought that, however mysterious God's standing afar off might be, by and by, when He drew nigh again, He would deal out even-handed justice to all; but such comfort is not open to those who explicitly deny God's remoteness, but on the contrary assert that He is the Presence from which there is no escaping. And the fact of evil, physical and moral, is precisely the chief and most fruitful source of religious scepticism; it is not the abstract question whether there is a God, but the practical and insistent problem whether the Divine goodness can be reconciled with the facts of life and experience, that is agitating men's minds, and sways their decision for or against religion.

Everyone knows that this is what Mr. Mallock some time ago called "the crux of Theism"; that "crux," to use his own language, is not "the existence of intelligent purpose in the universe," which may be freely conceded, but whether the processes of nature are or are not consistent with "a God possessing the character which it is the essence of Theism to attribute to Him, and which alone could render Him an object of religion, or even of interest, to mankind." Sometimes in accents of wistful wonder, sometimes in tones of revolt and defiant unbelief, the question is asked:—Why does God allow dire calamity, painful disease, earthquakes and shipwrecks, and accidents of the mine? Why does He permit war, or vivisection, or poverty, or vice—in fact any of "the heartache and the thousand natural shocks that flesh is heir to"? We should stop these things if we could; why does not He? One is reminded of Mr. William Watson's passionate arraignment of the Powers of Europe at the time of the Armenian massacres:—

> Yea, if ye could not, though ye would, lift hand—
> Ye halting leaders—to abridge Hell's reign...
> If such your plight, most hapless ye of men!
> *But if ye could and would not*, oh, what plea,
> Think ye, shall stead you at your trial, when
> The thundercloud of witnesses shall loom
> At the Assizes of Eternity?

The application of these burning lines is painfully obvious. It would be a positive relief were it thinkable that the Eternal would, but cannot, stem

> the flood that rolls Hoarser with
> anguish as the ages roll;

or if one might, with a modern novelist, compare the case to that of "a practitioner doing his best for a wilful patient, with poor appliances and indifferent nursing." *But if He could and will not—oh, what plea?*

What frankly appals men and freezes the worshipful instinct in their hearts is the apparent Divine indifference, the silence of God, in the presence of so much human wretchedness. If one could only feel that He cared for and sympathised with His suffering creatures, it would be a help, like the sympathetic pressure of the hand from a friend, which does not lessen the actual calamity that may have befallen us, but makes it easier to bear; but an *indifferent* God is equivalent to no God at all—or, as we have previously expressed it, a God who does not care, does not count. The mere sense that He was sorry for us would lighten the stroke of fate which He had not been able to avert; but if the truth is that He might have averted it by the simple exercise of His will, but refused to do so, coldly looking on at our grief—not from afar, but close by—then we can only say that no God at all were better than that. It seems, then, as though, in order to escape from palpable inconsistency between theory and fact, we should have to make a surrender either of His immanence, or His omnipotence, or His benevolence, or the reality of evil.

To surrender the Divine immanence will not really solve our problem. Near or far, closer to us than breathing or dwelling beyond the furthest star, God is still the Author of our being, the Framer of the world and all that therein is, the Cause without which there would have been no effects. If, after creating the world, He withdrew from it to an inconceivable distance, it is none the less His handiwork; if it is in and through His absence that the cosmic mechanism has got out of gear, it is yet He who willed to be so absent, well knowing what results would supervene; if a power other than He and hostile to Him has usurped the place and title of Prince of this world, such usurpation would have been impossible but for His acquiescence, and personified Evil, playing with human happiness, would still be His licensed agent. Evidently, the solution of which we are in search does not lie along that way.

We turn, therefore, to the second possible explanation, strongly put forward by Mill, according to whom natural theology points to God as "a Being of great but limited power."

Those who have been strengthened in goodness by relying on the sympathising support of a powerful and good Governor of the world (he says) have, I am satisfied, never really believed that Governor to be, in the strict sense of the term, omnipotent. They have always saved His goodness at the expense of His power. They have believed . . . that the world is inevitably imperfect, contrary to His intention.[1]

To the question, "Of what nature is the limitation of His power?" he returns the tentative answer that it

> probably results either from the qualities of the material—the substances and forces of which the universe is composed not admitting of any arrangements by which His purposes could be more completely fulfilled; or else, the purposes might have been more fully attained, but the Creator did not know how to do it; creative skill, wonderful as it is, was not sufficiently perfect to accomplish His purposes more thoroughly.[2]

Such an answer, we need scarcely say, could only have been given by a thinker who had grown up in the intellectual atmosphere of Deism; the Deity which he contemplates is One who works upon the world purely *ab extra*, who cannot be spoken of as the Creator, except by courtesy; in reality He merely shapes and adapts materials over which He has only an incomplete control, and which, therefore, so far from having been called into being by Him, must be thought of as existing independently of Him. Had He really *created* the raw material from which He was to frame the universe, He would of course have created some medium perfectly plastic to His hand and adapted to His purposes; but if He merely operates on matter from without, finding it stubborn and unamenable, He is only a secondary Deity or Demiurge, and we have still to answer the question, What is that real First Cause, the *Urgott* who created the *Urstoff*, matter in its most elementary form, and endowed it with qualities some of which were destined to serve, while others resisted and frustrated, the sub-Divinity's intentions?

Clearly, this notion also will not do; but while we may reject Mill's theory as to the *nature* of the limitations of Divine power, there is distinct force in his shrewd contention that religious people generally—professions to the contrary notwithstanding—have never really believed God to be, in the strict sense of the term, omnipotent. This contention we believe, indeed, to be almost self-evidently true; for on the contrary supposition nothing can happen contrary to God's will—all things and beings would necessarily be carrying out that will, and sin, *e.g.*, would become an utterly meaningless term. But if omnipotence is limited—which sounds, we admit, a contradiction in terms—we ask once more, In what way and by whom? To that question we have no other reply than the one given in our first chapter, *viz.*, that when we predicate limitation of the Deity, we must mean self-limitation. In creating the universe, we said, God made a distinction between His creation and Himself, and to that extent limited His Being—for the universe is not identical with God; we now add that in endowing man with an existence related to, but distinct from, His own, He limited not only His infinite Being, but also His infinite Power, delegating some portion thereof to us—for man's will is not identical with God's will, but capable of resisting, though also capable of co-operating with it. Without such individual initiative, without such an individual faculty of choosing between alternatives of action, man could never have been a moral agent; but moral liberty to choose and act aright or amiss implies also moral responsibility for such choice on the part of the chooser.

This neglected truth of God's self-limitation of His power needs to be far more explicitly avowed than has generally been the case. Only so shall we get clear of the confusion and uncertainty with which the subject of human freedom is so largely surrounded; only so shall we be enabled to place the burden of responsibility for sin, the cause of so immense a proportion of the world's suffering, upon the right shoulders—*i.e.*, man's, not God's. It is urgently necessary to disperse the common fallacy according to which God, being the Author of all, is the causative Agent answerable for all the happenings in His universe, for all human pain and all human sin. Where freedom is, *there* is responsibility. For let us bring the matter down from the abstract to the concrete: if a dreadful railway accident is caused through the momentary mental lapse of a signalman who has been overtaxed by excessive working hours, how is the responsibility God's? It obviously belongs to those who imposed a task involving the safety of human lives on a man who was not in a fit condition to fulfil such a duty. If an explosion in a coal-mine, accompanied by terrible loss of life, is caused through some miner striking a match, or carrying a naked light, in defiance of well-known regulations of safety, how is God responsible? He has endowed us with intelligence whereby to discover His laws, and with freedom to obey or disobey them: the use or misuse of that freedom rests with ourselves.

But now it may be asked—Was it the act of a benevolent Deity to entrust this terribly two-edged weapon of liberty to our unskilful hands, in which it was bound to work so vast an amount of injury? And this opens up the larger and more general question, Must we, in view of the facts of life, surrender the idea of the Divine benevolence? It is quite true that the evidence of purpose discernible in the whole structure of the universe proclaims the Deity to be personal; but, as Mr. Mallock says, "the theistic doctrine of God is not a doctrine that the supreme mind acts with purpose, but a doctrine that it acts with purpose of a highly specialised kind"—*viz.*, *benevolent* purpose.

Let us once more state the problem in the partial but very pertinent form in which it arises in connection with man's faculty of freedom. To bestow upon His creatures a gift which He must have known they would use in such a manner as to work infinite harm to themselves and to each other, seems *prima facie* no more compatible with kindly intentions than it would be to leave children to play with sharp tools, loaded firearms and deadly poisons; since disaster was bound to ensue from such a course, does not responsibility for the disaster rest with the one who deliberately provided the elements for it? But such a comparison, while superficially plausible, upon reflection is seen to be beside the mark. We really cannot plead such inexperience of right and wrong, such ignorance of moral safety and moral danger, as would furnish a true parallel between playing with temptation and playing with cyanide of potassium. In setting before us "life and good, and death and evil," God has as distinctly placed within our hearts the moral intuition which, says, "Therefore choose life." But why, the questioner proceeds, have made sin even possible? Because, we answer, not to have done so would have made morality impossible. It cannot be too often, or too plainly, pointed out that just as the only alternative to purpose is chance, so the only alternative to liberty is necessity. That is to say, God could no doubt have made us automata instead of free agents; but even He could not have made us free to *choose* the right, yet not free to choose its contrary. Choice that is not willed is not choice at all; goodness by compulsion is not goodness, but merely correctitude—the behaviour of a skilfully-devised mechanism, but possessing no *moral* quality whatever. We are not at present concerned with the view of those who maintain that men are *de facto* no more than such "cunning casts in clay" a contention which will occupy us at a later stage; we merely state the commonplace that in making us free God Himself could not also make us impeccable, insusceptible to temptation, immune against the possibility of sin.

The real question, then, shapes itself as follows: Can we discern the nature of the purpose which expresses itself in the bestowal of this gift of freedom? Stated in that form, we see that the question has already been answered by implication; for if there could be no morality without liberty, it is fair to make the inference that the very object of God in allowing us to choose between alternatives of conduct was to make morality so much as possible. Was that a good and beneficent object? We submit that even those who impeach the Deity for opening the door to sin would on second thoughts confess that morally free—and therefore peccable—beings stand on a higher level than marionettes, however faultlessly contrived to perform certain evolutions. The truth of the matter is set forth with poetic insight in Andersen's story of the Nightingale—the immeasurable difference between the artificial bird and the real songster, whose melodious raptures somehow touched a chord in the listener which all the nicely-calculated trills and cadences of the ingenious mechanical toy failed to set in motion. In like manner we repeat that the power to determine his own course raises man to a plane incomparably higher than he could have occupied as an automaton. The same faculty of free choice which in its abuse makes the sinner, in its right exercise furnishes forth the saint. All that we mean by moral progress, by "the steady gain of man," his rise to more exalted ideals, his conquest of baser appetites—all that makes the history of the race a thrilling and uplifting drama—is bound up with his possession of liberty; it is this supreme gift which makes him "a little lower than the angels," and "crowns him with glory and honour." Alone of all earthly beings, man is not only an effect but a cause; his freedom—not unlimited but quite real within its not inelastic confines—is the noblest of all his faculties, even though for that very reason it is capable of being most ignobly perverted. What its bestowal tells us is that God does not call us into servitude, but to that service which is perfect freedom; He might have made us His playthings, as Plato suggested,[3] but by endowing us with the power to choose for ourselves He has made us His potential fellow-workers. May we not ask—Who, after all, would prefer the safety of automatism to the glory of this Divine adventure?

In all this we are not shutting our eyes to what is involved in the misuse of liberty—the dread nature of wilful sin and its ghastly harvest of wrecked and ruined lives; we do not say that the price of freedom is not a heavy one, nor do we pretend that the subject is free from painful mystery. It could not be otherwise; that we, with our limited vision and circumscribed understanding, should be able to solve that mystery with any completeness, is not even to be imagined. Nevertheless, we may claim that we have at least obtained a glimpse of the purpose of God in conferring upon the race this fateful power; for this and no other was the appointed means by which man was to ascend to his true place as a moral and spiritual being. If we can admit that purpose to be in harmony with the Divine benevolence, we may the more hopefully turn to other aspects of our problem.

[1] *Three Essays on Religion*, p. 22.

[2] *Ibid*, p. 79.

[3] *The Laws*, vii, 803: [Greek] "Theou ti paignion memechanmenon." Compare also Browning's unhappy phrase, "God, whose puppets, best and worst, are we."

CHAPTER VII

EVIL *versus* DIVINE GOODNESS (*Continued*)

There is probably no more serious aspect of the popular philosophy which declares so confidently, "There is no will that is not God's will," than that, while professing to be a Gospel of sweetness and light, it in reality plunges us into the very depths of pessimism by making God Himself "ultimately responsible for all the evil and suffering in the world." From such a position, from such premises as these, there is only one step to such conclusions as have been actually drawn:—

It is His world, remember; He made it, and He is omnipotent. . . If creation does not please the Creator, why did He not make it better? If it is wayward and intractable, it can be no more than He expected, or ought to have expected. Wherein consists His right to punish us for our transgressions? Suppose we challenge it; what will He say in defence?

We may shrink with distaste from such wild and whirling words; but if it be true that "there is no will that is not God's will"—if whatever takes place in the universe expresses that almighty will—they are as rational in their very vehemence as Omar's lines are rational in their melancholy:—

> O Thou, who didst with pitfall and with gin
> Beset the Road I was to wander in,
>   Thou wilt not with Predestin'd Evil round
> Enmesh, and then impute my Fall to Sin!
>
> O Thou, who man of baser Earth didst make,
> And ev'n with Paradise devise the Snake:
>   For all the Sin wherewith the Face of Man
> Is blacken'd—Man's forgiveness give—and take!

It is only when we clearly recognise that man is other than a mere phase or mode of the one Eternal Being; that he has been endowed with individual existence and individual will, and therefore with individual responsibility—and that for the express purpose of realising his highest potentialities: it is only when we accept such a reading of the facts as this that we escape from that worst of nightmares which reaches its climax in hurling its foolish defiance at the Most High, challenging His right to punish the instruments of His own will, those "helpless pieces of the game He plays," impotent items in that unending spectacle—

Which for the pastime of Eternity
He doth Himself contrive, enact, behold.

But if it is true that God bestowed freedom upon us because only as free agents could we learn to love and do the right for its own sake; if it is true that the struggle which we have to wage against our lower impulses has the wholly benevolent object of enabling us to achieve the glory of a perfected character, it has also to be borne in mind that under no circumstances can character be conceived otherwise than as the "result" of growth. That is to say, God Himself could not call moral perfection into being ready-made, by a mere *fiat*, and that for the same reason which precludes omnipotence itself from making two straight lines to enclose a space, *i.e.*, because the idea involves a self-contradiction. So true is this that we read even of our Saviour that "though He was a Son, yet He learned obedience by the things which He suffered," and in this manner was "made perfect." Character in its very definition is the result of many deliberate exercises of a free will; and if the evolution of character was an object dearer to God than the highest mechanical or animal perfection, that object could have been secured in no other way than by this particular endowment.

And here we shall also find the reply to the very natural inquiry why God does not, as He might, intervene or frustrate the evil designs of wrong-doers. Why does a good God allow His intentions to be set at defiance by those whom the prophet described as drawing iniquity with cords of vanity, and sin as it were with a cart rope? It would not matter so much, we sometimes bitterly reflect, if the sinner injured only himself by his wickedness; but how often are the innocent made to suffer by the devices of the unscrupulous and selfish! Why, we repeat, this strange non-intervention of the Most High on behalf of His own cause? On this it must be remarked in the first place that those who accept God's transcendence will be careful not to rule out *a priori* the possibility of such Divine action as, regarded from our point of view, would have to be described as intervention; the question whether such action has ever taken place, is a question of fact, and the view that at particular junctures God has thus actively "intervened" is at any rate capable of being strongly argued. But admitting, as we think we must, that ordinary life does not show any instances of such supernatural interposition—that a reckless financier is allowed to enrich himself by cornering the wheat supply and sending up the price of the people's bread; that a band of reactionaries may arrest the course of reform and plunge a country back into darkness; that a beneficent act of the legislature may be defeated by greedy cunning—must we despair of solving the general problem which such cases suggest?

We think, on the contrary, that the explanation may be legitimately sought in what we conceive to have been the Divine intention in making man free;

that intention, the making of character, would obviously suffer defeat by God throwing His weight—if we may use such a phrase—into this scale as against that, furthering here and checking there, for character, as we just said, can only result from the free exercise and interplay of will with will. We may well imagine God's mode of action to resemble that of a human parent who entrusts a growing child with a growing measure of liberty and responsibility, well knowing that in the use of it he will have many a slip and stumble, and occasionally hurt himself; such a parent will carefully refrain from interference, preferring that the child should learn his own lessons from his own mistakes, well knowing that we profit only by the experience for which we ourselves have paid. No one will, of course, pretend that such a reconciliation of the facts of sin with the axiom or intuition of Divine all-goodness is other than incomplete; we merely urge that, having regard to the magnitude and the complexity of the subject it could not be otherwise. A theory, without accounting for all the facts, may be true so far as it goes, correctly indicating the way which, if we could pursue it further, would lead us into more and fuller truth. No doubt, when that which is perfect is come, that which is in part will be done away; but pending the advent of a complete explanation, a partial one is not without all value.

Indeed, the very inadequacy of our instruments, resulting in that incompleteness of which we just spoke, should once more suggest a reflection which, while in no wise original or startling, is specially relevant to the subject under discussion: for if God's knowledge necessarily and immeasurably transcends ours, if He knows *more* than we, does it not follow with equal certainty that He knows *better*? Granted that we do not understand how this or that dispensation of Providence fits in with the general belief in His perfect goodness, our failure to understand no more disproves that goodness than the similar failure of a child to comprehend why such and such irksome tasks are imposed upon him by his parent, disproves the wisdom and goodness which prompt the parent's act. The child *cannot* understand; but where the relations are at all normal he acquiesces, being on general grounds convinced that the parental commands aim at his welfare, and that his parents, after all, know better than he. Is the application so far to seek?

In the second place—turning now from the subject of sin to that of evil generally—it may be worth while to remind ourselves of a fact which seems to be forgotten by some of the impetuous arraigners of the Deity, *viz.*, that, after all, the problem is not a new one, which they have suddenly discovered by dint of superior sagacity. What we mean is this: the problem of evil as such is of anything but an abstruse or remote nature, nor one requiring unusual philosophical penetration to bring to light; on the contrary, pain and sorrow, privation, adversity, death—these are experiences that have come within the cognisance of all. If, then, the facts are neither so remote nor so inconsiderable that men could have simply forgotten to take them into account in framing their estimates of the Divine character, how is it, we ask, that they have arrived at and clung to the belief in the benevolence of God at all? If the proof to the contrary was so overpowering, why, as a matter of fact, has it *not* overpowered them? Why should an unknown Hebrew singer have given expression to this extraordinary sentiment, "Though He slay me, yet will I trust in Him"—and why has that sentiment been re-echoed by millions of men and women acquainted with grief and affliction? The early Christians did not exactly live lives of luxury or even security, sheltered from contact with tragedy and horror; yet the keynote of primitive Christianity is the note of joy, while the background of early Christian experience is a radiant conviction of the Divine benevolence. And when we remember that the same holds true of so many eminently spiritual souls in all ages, who have combined a keen sensitiveness to evil and suffering of every kind with an unshakeable trust in the lovingkindness of God, we shall scarcely accuse all this cloud of witnesses of having simply drugged themselves and refused to accept the evidence of their own senses. If men and women suffering from anything rather than moral blindness or moral anaesthesia could, and can, nevertheless believe with all their hearts in the Divine Fatherhood, is not such a recurring circumstance significant in itself? Evidently, granting all the facts, more than one reading of the facts is possible; not cloistered mystics, or anchorites withdrawn from the world, but heroes engaged in fighting its ills, have steadfastly proclaimed that God is good; is it an altogether unreasonable hypothesis that their faith, if it outsoars ours, may be the result of a deeper insight?

And this, in turn, suggests another thought, simple enough in itself, yet not always borne in mind in connection with this particular theme—*viz.*, that we are never dealing with facts *per se*, but with facts *plus* our interpretation of them, which may be right or wrong, but which, right or wrong, helps to decide in a very large measure what the facts themselves shall mean to us. Our attitude towards the events which befall us makes all the difference. If men have been ruined by success, it is as true that men have been made by failure. If men have deteriorated through ease and plenty, men have been stimulated to effort through hardship and poverty. In a word, if there is much in the burden, there is as much in the shouldering. But for Dante's consecration of sorrow, the world would have lost the *Commedia Divina*. But for a painful and permanently disabling accident, the English Labour Movement would not have had one of its principal leaders in Mr. Philip Snowden. And as for the influence of outward events and environment generally, Mr. Chesterton may exaggerate in suggesting that everything good has been snatched from some catastrophe, but he is certainly right when he says that "the most dangerous environment of all is the commodious environment." On the other hand, of an environment the reverse of commodious, it has been observed:—

Logic would seem to say, "If God brings great pain on a man, it must make the man revolt against God." But observation of facts compels us to say, "No, on the contrary, nothing exercises so extraordinary an influence in making men love God as the suffering of great pain at His hands." Scientific thinking deals with facts as they are, not with *a priori* notions of what we should expect. And in this matter, the fact as it is, is that goodness is evolved from pain more richly than from any other source.[1]

We may think such a statement too absolute, and point to cases where the effect of physical suffering has been altogether different; but if it is true that in certain well-authenticated and not merely exceptional instances such visitations have resulted in strengthened faith and heightened goodness, our main contention is proved, namely, that the attitude of the individual himself towards the events of his life has much to do with determining what those events are to mean to him. Instead of "Was the gift good?" we should more often ask, "Was the recipient wise?" Pain is pain, and disaster is disaster; but the spirit in which we meet them matters immensely.

But now we are confronted with a more fundamental question: Could not God have obviated the phenomenon of pain altogether? Could He not have made us incapable of feeling any but pleasant sensations? Mill, who in his essay on *Nature* devotes some—for him—almost vehement pages to this subject, reaches the conclusion that "the only admissible moral theory of Creation is that the Principle of Good *cannot* at once and altogether subdue the powers of evil" [2]; and in dealing with the same topic in the essay on *Theism*, while admitting that "appearances do not indicate that contrivance was brought into play purposely to produce pain," he holds to the view that its very existence shows the power of God to be limited *ab extra*, by the material conditions under which He works:—

The author of the machinery is no doubt accountable for having made it susceptible to pain; but this may have been a necessary condition of its susceptibility to pleasure; a supposition which avails nothing on the theory of an omnipotent Creator, but is an extremely probable one in the case of a Contriver working under the limitation of inexorable laws and indestructible properties of matter.[3]

Such a view of the case, as we have already said in our previous chapter, is purely deistic; but we must now proceed to point out, with great respect for so great an intellect as Mill's, that the supposition which, he says, "avails nothing on the theory of an omnipotent Creator"—*viz.*, that susceptibility to pleasure involves susceptibility to pain—seems to us to fit and cover the facts precisely; for a capacity for pain and a capacity for pleasure are not two different things which could conceivably exist apart from each other, but are only different manifestations of one and the same capacity, *viz.*, for experiencing sensations of any kind whatsoever. We could no more be capable of feeling pleasure, while _in_capable of feeling pain, than we could be sensitive to musical harmonies, while _in_sensible to musical discords; besides which, monotony of sensation annihilates sensation. On this point we may invoke against the pre-evolutionist Mill a modern scientific authority like Professor Fiske, who expresses himself to the effect that "without the element of antagonism there could be no consciousness, and therefore no world." "It is not a superficial but a fundamental truth," he observes, "that if there were no colour but red, it would be exactly the same thing as if there were no colour at all. . . If our ears were to be filled with one monotonous roar of Niagara, unbroken by alien sounds, the effect upon consciousness would be absolute silence. If our palates had never come in contact with any tasteful thing save sugar, we should know no more of sweetness than of bitterness. If we had never felt physical pain, we could not recognise physical pleasure. For want of the contrasted background, its pleasurableness would cease to exist. . . We are thus brought to a striking conclusion, the essential soundness of which cannot be gainsaid. *In a happy world there must be sorrow and pain.*" [4] And this necessity, we would add, does not follow from God's failure to overcome any "inexorable laws and indestructible properties *of matter*," but is implied in the inexorable laws *of thought*—in that eternal right reason which makes it impossible for Deity to do what is self-contradictory or absurd.

But if the necessity of pain be thus admitted—a most important admission—we may now take a step further ahead. Even Mill, as we just saw, expressly disclaimed the notion of attributing physical evil to malign intention on the Creator's part; what separates us from Mill is that in our view the laws of nature, in inflicting pain, do not act independently of God, but are His laws. Do those, it may be asked, who allege His "indifference" in not interfering with the operation of the forces of nature when they injure us, frame a very clear notion of the way in which they think that God should, or might, manifest His "interest"? On reflection it will be found that what they ask for—the only possible alternative to an unbroken natural order—is such constant miraculous interposition as would make that order non-existent. But assuming that there were no regular sequence or uniformity to speak of—if we never knew whether the course of nature might not be interrupted at any moment on somebody's behalf—should we really be so much better off? Would humanity be happier if chaos was substituted for order? Without seeking to mitigate the suffering entailed by the unhindered action of nature's forces, it is still certain that the sheer confusion of a world in which law had been abrogated would be infinitely worse. Indeed, this is to understate the case; for the fact is that in such a world all the activities of life would be completely paralysed, and hence life itself, as we have already had occasion to point out, could not be carried on. But if the reign of natural law thus represents the only set of conditions under which life is even possible; and if at the same time this law, which operates all the time and never relaxes its hold, is the expression of the will of God, how can we charge Him with indifference? The truth is, on the contrary, that He is exercising His care, not intermittently, by performing a miracle whenever things go wrong, but continually, and without any interruption whatsoever. Were His law other than steadfast, were there occasional or frequent departures from it, were it possible to defy nature with impunity just now and again, the results of such irregular action would be disastrous in the extreme; it is because His will is constant, and His decrees without variableness, that we are able to learn and obey them, and by obeying to master nature.

"But, after all, He made the laws, and He could have made different ones." Certainly; but a moment's reflection will show that He could not have made laws of *any* kind, disobedience to which would have had the same consequences as obedience. He might—for all we can say to the contrary—have made strychnine nutritious, and wheat deadly to us; but even in that case an indulgence in wheat would have brought about the unpleasant effects at present associated with an overdose of *nux vomica*. He might have made a raw, damp atmosphere, with easterly winds, the most conducive to health; but even then it would have been rash to take up one's residence in a warm, dry climate. Pain is an indication that the processes of life are suffering some more or less serious disturbance; given, therefore, any set of natural laws, and the necessity of obeying them as the condition of life itself, and we see that disobedience to them would always and inevitably mean pain. We repeat that God might have made different laws; but whatever they were, their breach must have recoiled upon the breaker.

Yet even if reflections like these demonstrate to us the necessity for pain, we are still left to face those greater calamities and disasters which sweep away human lives by the hundred and thousand, catastrophes like the Sicilian earthquakes, that are marked by an appalling wantonness of destruction; must not such events as these also be attributed to God, and how are they to be reconciled with His alleged benevolence? Certainly, no one would attempt to minimise the horrors of the Sicilian tragedy; the human mind is overwhelmed by the suddenness, no less than the magnitude, of an upheaval of nature resulting in the blotting-out of whole flourishing communities. And yet we venture to say, paradoxical though it sounds, that it is, partly at least, owing to a certain lack of imagination that such an event looms so immense in our thoughts. Most of us do not make the ordinance of death in itself an accusation against the Most High; we are not specially shocked or outraged by the thought that the whole population of the globe dies out within quite a moderate span of time, nor even by the reflection that several hundred thousand persons die every year in the United Kingdom alone. We know quite well that every one of those who perished in Messina must have paid his debt to nature in, at most, a few decades. So, then, the whole point in our arraignment is this—It would not have been cruel had these deaths been spread over a period of time, but it is cruel that they should have taken place simultaneously; it would not have been cruel had the victims of the earthquake died of illnesses—in many cases prolonged and painful—but it is cruel that death should have come upon them swiftly, instantaneously, without menace or lingering pain; it would not have been cruel had children survived to mourn their parents, husbands their wives, brother the loss of brother, as in the ordinary course—but it is cruel that by dying in the same hour they were spared the pang of parting. We repeat that it is because we ordinarily use our imaginations too little that we are so apt to lose our balance and sense of proportion in the presence of these catastrophes; and it may be permissible to point out that there is probably, quality for quality, and quantity for quantity, more grey, hopeless suffering, more wretchedness and tragedy, in London to-day than was caused by the Sicilian catastrophe—suffering and wretchedness that are due not to nature, but to sin, though not necessarily on the sufferer's part.

And there is, in justice, something more to be said when we speak of these dire visitations. While every instinct of humanity inspires us with sympathy for the victims buried under the ruins of Messina and Reggio, it is, of course, a matter of common knowledge that the soil on those coasts is volcanic, and liable to such commotions; if men will take the risk of living in such localities, we may pity them when the disaster comes, but we cannot very fitly impeach Providence. There is a village near Chur in Switzerland, which has twice been wiped out by avalanches, yet each time re-built on the same spot; year by year material is visibly accumulating for a third deadly fall, and when it takes place, as take place it will, men will speak of the dispassionate cruelty of nature. Time after time the lava from Mount Vesuvius has overwhelmed the localities that nestle on its slopes, but human heedlessness proves incurable. If the Sicilians, knowing the nature of the soil, had built their towns of isolated, one-storied, wooden structures, at a reasonable distance from the shore, the effects of earthquake and tidal wave would not have been one hundredth part as terrible; yet Messina is being re-built on its former site, and apparently in the old style of architecture—a proceeding which simply invites a repetition of the same kind of disaster. It is literally true that these greater calamities are in nearly every instance capable of being averted or their incidence minimised; to give an obvious instance, one is almost weary of seeing it repeated that the famines and consequent epidemics which visit India could be immensely reduced by a wise and generous expenditure on irrigation, the improved cultivation of the land, the enlargement of the cultivable area, and so forth. But men find it easier to turn accusing glances to the sky than to bestir themselves and to use more wisdom, foresight and energy in directing and subduing the forces of nature.

We are well aware that what has been written in the pages of this chapter is no more than a series of scattered hints; we do not for a moment imagine that, in the aggregate, they amount to more than a most fragmentary resolution of the difficulty presented by the reality of evil—indeed, we have already expressed our belief that a full solution must in the nature of things lie beyond our ken. But if it should appear from the foregoing considerations that some aspects of our problem—such as the existence of sin and of pain—are not as irreconcilable with the goodness of God as may have seemed to be the case, reflection should lead us to the reasonable hope that if we understood more, we should receive fuller and fuller proof of the truth that God is Love. And when we remember that that Love shines out most brightly from the Cross, and that the world's greatest tragedy has been the world's greatest blessing, the turning-point in the history of the race, we may well hush our impatience, refrain over-confident criticisms, and commit ourselves to the Father's hands even while we can only see His purposes as in a glass, darkly. We may believe, with the psalmist of old, that by and by we "shall behold His face in *righteousness*; we shall be satisfied, when we awake, with His likeness."

[1] R. A. Armstrong, *God and the Soul*, pp. 161-162.

[2] *Op. cit.*, p. 21.

[3] *Ibid*, p. 82.

[4] *Through Nature to God*, pp. 36, 37.

CHAPTER VIII
THE DENIAL OF EVIL

We closed our last chapter with a confession and an appeal—a confession of the incompleteness of our answers to the questions suggested by the fact of evil, and an appeal for patience in recognising that that incompleteness is inevitable, having regard to our constitutional limitations. "There is," as Newman said, "a certain grave acquiescence in ignorance, a recognition of our impotence to solve momentous and urgent questions, which has a satisfaction of its own." [1] That, however, is an attitude to which all will not resign themselves. If a knot cannot be unravelled, their one idea of what to do is to cut it; if evil cannot be explained, it can at any rate be denied. Thus we find a distinguished living essayist, with a large constituency of cultured readers, writing as follows:—

The essence of God's omnipotence is that both law and matter are His and originate from Him; so that if a single fibre of what we know to be evil can be found in the world, either God is responsible for that, or He is dealing with something He did not originate and cannot overcome. Nothing can extricate us from this dilemma, except that what we think evil is not really evil at all, but hidden good.

If the views of Divine power and responsibility set forth in this book are true—if, *i.e.*, we are justified in having recourse to a theory of Divine self-limitation—it will be clear that Mr. Benson's "dilemma" is, to say the least, overstated; but were that dilemma as desperate as he depicts it, it has strangely escaped him that his suggested mode of extrication is more desperate still. For what he asks us to do is quite simply to abdicate our judgment in respect of both physical and ethical phenomena—not merely to withhold our decision upon this or that particular occurrence, but to admit in general terms that evil is only apparent and not real. But see to what such an admission commits us: if we have no grounds for saying that evil is evil, we can have no grounds either for saying that good is good; if our faculties are incompetent to diagnose the one kind of phenomena accurately, they cannot be any more competent to diagnose and deliver reliable verdicts upon the other kind. It is quite a mistake to think that by getting rid of the reality of evil we preserve or affirm the more emphatically the reality of good; if we confidently pronounce our experience of evil an illusion, what value can there attach to our finding that our experience of its opposite is a fact? Such is the Nemesis which waits on remedies of the "heroic" order.

Nevertheless this particular remedy seems to be enjoying a considerable popularity at the present time; indeed, in discussing some aspects of the doctrine which affirms the "allness" of God, and the allied one of Monism, we have already seen that where these are professed, evil must be explicitly or implicitly denied. This denial is common to the various confused movements—all of them the outcome of a misconceived idealism—which under the names of "New Thought," "Higher Thought," "Joy Philosophy," "Christian Science," etc., etc., find their disciples chiefly amongst that not inconsiderable section of the public which has been aptly described as dominated by a "longing to combine a picturesque certainty devoid of moral discipline with unlimited transcendental speculations." All these cults combine a vague optimism with an extravagant subjectivity; all would have us believe that so far from things being what they are, they are whatever we may think them to be; all with one accord treat evil in its various manifestations as unreal, and maintain, as it has been neatly phrased, that "the process of cure lies in the realisation that there is nothing to be cured." The attraction of such a doctrine for that large number of persons who dislike strenuous effort—either intellectual or moral—is easily accounted for. Evil as a fact is not conducive to the comfort of those who contemplate it—how pleasant to be told that it exists only in disordered imaginations; the sense of sin has always interfered with the enjoyment of life—what a relief to learn that it is merely a chimaera; pain is grievous indeed—what benefactors are those who teach us how to conjure it away by the simple process of declaring that there is no such thing! A creed promising to accomplish such desirable objects could be sure of votaries, if proclaimed with sufficient *aplomb*; here, we may surmise, is the main explanation of the welcome given to those monistic ethics to which we referred in an earlier chapter, and of the vogue of so-called "Christian Science," which invites consideration as the most typical and important of a whole group of movements.

We repeat that the nature of the Christian Science appeal largely explains the rapid spread of this cult. Christian Science is quite unlike other religions in this, that while they promise at most salvation—an intangible boon—Mrs. Eddy promises her followers *health*, relief from bodily pain and sickness, and thus addresses herself to a universally and urgently felt want. A merely spiritual message may fail to obtain listeners; but—to state the truth baldly—a person need not be particularly spiritually-minded in order to be drawn towards Christian Science. The natural man would much rather be made well than made good, and a creed which professes to be able to do the former will touch him in his most sensitive part. Certainly, this was one of the difficulties of Christ's public ministry, *viz.*, that the people flocked to Him to be cured rather than to be taught. But while He declined to place the emphasis on His works of healing—while He left Capernaum by

Himself before sunrise in order to escape the importunities of the mob, and refused Peter's request that He should return thither with the words, "Let us go elsewhere into the next towns that I may preach there also; for to *this* end came I forth"—Christian Science addresses its sure appeal to man's material nature. The contrast is significant.

And yet the true essence of Christian Science is not "faith-healing" in the ordinary sense. It does not say, *e.g.*, "Here is a case of genuine, unmistakeable rheumatism or consumption, but faith is able to dispel it"; on the contrary, it says, "This alleged rheumatism or consumption is a mere illusion, a phantasm of the imagination; and the way to be cured is for the 'patient' to discover his mistake. There are no maladies—there are only *malades imaginaires*." Mrs. Eddy states in plain words that "Mortal ills are but errors of thought" [2]; it is from this point of view that Christian Science as a system has to be approached and understood.

With the fantastic exegesis of Scripture on which this creed professes to be based, we are not directly concerned; else something might be said of the method of interpretation which is to be found in the official text-book of the movement—a method which sees in the serpent the symbol of malicious animal magnetism, which identifies the Holy Ghost and the New Jerusalem with Christian Science, and the little book brought down from heaven by the mighty angel with Mrs. Eddy's own *magnum opus*, *Science and Health*. As Mr. Podmore drily remarks, "In these holy games each player is at liberty to make words mean what he wants them to mean"; at the same time, these grotesque and arbitrary constructions are not precisely calculated to inspire the confidence of balanced minds.

Let us, however, turn at once to the fundamental axioms of Christian Science:—

(1) God is All in all.

(2) God is Good. Good is Mind.

(3) God, Spirit, being all, nothing is matter.

(4) Life, God, Omnipotent Good, deny death, evil, sin, disease.

In other words, Christian Science begins—and, for the matter of that, ends—with the categorical statement that the one and only Reality is Mind, Goodness, God, all three of which terms it uses synonymously and interchangeably. So much being granted, the rest follows "in a concatenation according"; the possible permutations are many—the result is always one. *God is All*: hence, says Mrs. Eddy, "*All is God*, and there is naught beside Him"; but *God is Good*, and as He is *All*, it follows that *All is Good*; and if all is good, *there can be no evil*. Again, Mrs. Eddy propounds the following three propositions: *God is Mind; Good is Mind; All is Mind*; therefore, once more, all is good, all is God, and *there can be no evil*. Or, to introduce another variation—*God is All*, and *God is Mind*; therefore *Mind is all*; therefore *there is no matter*. Grant the Christian Science premises, and there is no escaping the Christian Science conclusions.

But do we grant these premises—do we grant Mrs. Eddy's fundamental pantheistic assumption of "the allness of God" [3]? We have shown again and again why we do not; and with the rejection of the basal tenet of Christian Science the superstructure follows. But now let us show how all Mrs. Eddy's juggling with words, all her assertions of the goodness of all and the allness of good, do not help her to get rid of evil. Granting for argument's sake that Mind is the only reality, then the test of reality must be this—that something exists in or for a mind; in so far, then, as evil, pain, and so forth exist, as Christian Science tells us, "only" in some mind—in so far as "disease is a thing of thought" [4]—evil, pain, disease, etc., must *pro tanto* be real, nay, the most real of realities, for where except in mind could they exist? And even if we can successfully annihilate them by denying their existence, whence did they come in the first place? From "malicious animal magnetism"? But if God is All in all, and All-good, what is that malicious animal magnetism which is somehow not God and not good? Does not this whole tangle serve yet once more to illustrate the futility of that doctrine of Divine allness which we have seen successfully masquerading as Divine immanence?

Let us test the worth of these speculations in yet another way. Christian Science declares evil to be non-existent, illusory, an "error of thought." But that which is true of a species must be true of all its genera; if all men are mortal, and Socrates is a man, it follows that Socrates is mortal; if evil as a whole is nonexistent, that which applies to the general phenomenon must equally apply to each and all of its manifestations. But error is undoubtedly a form, and even a serious form, of evil; from which it would follow that if evil is not real, error is not possible—and in that case one opinion is as good as its opposite, and black and white are only different descriptions of the same thing. But if that is so, if one thing is as true as another, we shall conclude that, *e.g.*, the rejection of Christian Science is no more erroneous than its affirmation. Will Christian Scientists acquiesce in that inference? And if they will not, by what means do they propose to show that it is not a legitimate deduction from their own axiom, the unreality of evil? If error is a real fact, evil must be so to that extent; on the other hand, how can it be an error to believe that evil is real, if error, being an evil, must itself be illusory?

But it is time we turned from our examination of the principles of Christian Science to their application. So far as the wholesale declaration of the illusoriness of physical evil—the ravages and tortures of disease—is concerned, the implicit belief extended to the pretensions of this creed to master all such ills is proof, if proof were wanted, of the success which rewards those who act on the maxim, "*de l'audace, toujours de l'audace*!" Given the right kind and amount of faith, we are assured, Christian Science treatment will prove effective in a case of double pneumonia, or compound fracture, or malignant tumour, without the assistance of the physician—above all, without "drugs," which are pronounced *taboo* by Mrs. Eddy; "and that," to quote Mr. Podmore again, "is a postulate which can never be contradicted by experience, for failure can always be ascribed—as it is, in fact, ascribed by the Christian Scientist to-day—to want of faith or 'Science' on the part of the sufferer." Nothing could be more entirely simple or unanswerable: if the patient improves or recovers, the credit goes to Christian Science; if he gets worse or dies, the unfortunate result is debited to his lack of faith. The only thing Christian Science fails to answer is, as we have already seen, the preliminary question, *viz.*, what caused the disease—or at any rate the semblance, the malignant hallucination of disease—in the first instance. If God is all and all is God; if God is Mind and there is nothing but Mind; if all therefore is mind and all is good—whence in a good Mind comes even the hallucination of pain and evil? "The thoughts of the practitioner," says Mrs. Eddy, "should be imbued with a clear conviction of the omnipotence and omnipresence of God; . . . and hence, that whatever militates against health . . . is an unjust usurper of the throne of the Controller of all mankind." [5] But if God is omnipresent, His presence must be displayed in the disease; if He is omnipotent, how can there be a usurper on His throne? If He is All, how can there be aught beside Him? These are points on which we wait in vain for enlightenment from the Boston mysteriarch.

We shall be told, however, that whatever flaws there may be in the theory of Christian Science, this cult could not possibly have obtained its vogue if it were all promise and no performance; and as a matter of fact, testimonies to the curative effect of the treatment abound, furnished by those who say they have been restored to health by these methods, and as convincing as such testimony can be. We use the latter phrase advisedly; it is impossible to read these documents without being convinced of the entire good faith of the writers in relating what they themselves believe to be true; it is impossible not to be convinced by the perusal of their accounts that cures of some sort took place: the one thing of which it is possible to remain quite unconvinced is the fundamental contention of Christian Science, *viz.*, that there was no disease to be cured. Speaking quite generally, if one is going to be impressed by testimonials there is of course, no patent pill of respectable advertising power which cannot produce such by the wastepaper-basketful; and perfectly sincere and unsolicited testimonials, too. What these prove, however, is neither that the patients have been cured of the particular diseases they may name—and in the diagnosis of which they may very likely be mistaken—nor above all that it is the taking of a particular preparation to which they owe their cures; they prove the enormous power of suggestion and auto-suggestion, in virtue of which many ailments yield to the patient's firm assurance that by following a certain course he will get better. Everyone knows that a manner which inspires confidence, a happy blend of cheerfulness and suave authority, is of at least equal value to a physician as his skill and diplomas; and it is probably true, approximately at any rate, that a man can no more be cured of a serious illness unless he believes in his curability, than he can be hypnotised against his will. But between the recognition of such a fact, and the description of a cancer as an obstinate illusion, or a crushed limb as an "error of thought," there is just the difference which separates sanity from extravaganza.

In short, that which is of truth in Christian Science is not peculiar to it; while what is peculiar to its teaching, the denial of the reality of shattered legs, wasted lungs, diseased spines, etc., is not true. The power of mind over body, the possibility of healing certain diseases by suggestion, is not the discovery of Mrs. Eddy; the assumption on the other hand, that *all* diseases are susceptible to such treatment is characteristic of the school of which she is the latest and best-known representative—only it is false. "All physicians of broad practice and keen observation realise that certain pains may be alleviated or cured, and that certain morbid conditions may be made to disappear, provided a change in the mental state of the patient can be brought about. . . . It does not require special learning to build up a psychotherapeutic practice based upon the observation of such cases; and the Christian Science healers, narrowly educated and of narrow experience, have done just this thing, resting upon the theory that the mental influence of the healer is the effective curative agent. It is easy to see how a development of this theory would lead to the assumption that all kinds of diseases may be curable by mental influence emanating from a healer, this leading to the practice of the so-called 'absent-treatment,' with all its follies and dangers." [6] When it is added that the Christian Science healer is a professional person, and that the cost of "absent-treatment" may come to as much as ten dollars an hour, we need say no more about the "dangers" alluded to.[7] That the quasi-religious formulas of Christian Science may prove extremely effective in bringing about such a change in the mental state of certain patients as will cause pains to be alleviated or cured, and morbid conditions to disappear, one need have no hesitation in believing; moreover, as the medical author just quoted acutely observes, it is quite possible that some patients would not be cured unless they were "allowed to believe that their cures are due to some mysterious or miraculous agency." But even such an admission does not mean that Christian Science does more than apply the principle of suggestion, increasing its efficacy by utilising the religious faculty of the patient; nor, above all, does it give countenance to the root-contention of the creed, *viz.*, that pain and disease are unreal. Once more, if mind be the only reality, then pain, seeing that it can only be experienced by a mind, is real in exact proportion as it is intense.

It might seem unnecessary to add anything more to what has been said in refutation of the claims of Christian Science so far as physical healing is concerned; but one or two very simple considerations will complete our case without greatly detaining us.

In stating categorically and without qualification that "mortal ills are but errors of thought," Mrs. Eddy seems to have overlooked two classes of patients to whom it would be somewhat difficult to apply this sweeping generalisation. We wonder, for instance, how this theory could be made to cover the large category of infantile ailments. How, we are entitled to ask, would Christian Science deal with the teething-troubles which attend babyhood? Is it seriously suggested that a feverish, wailing child is merely the victim of an hallucination—and how would the Christian Scientist undertake to convince him of his illusion? On the face of it, such an enterprise does not look hopeful. But further, it so happens that human beings are not the only sufferers from pain and sickness; animals are subject to diseases, and often to the same diseases as men. We disclaim all intention of treating the subject otherwise than seriously—but if a man's rheumatism is an illusion, what causes the same affection in a dog or a chimpanzee? And if an embrocation may be used with good effects in the latter case, why may it not be used in the former? We need not press these questions; they will serve as they stand to show once more how this whole pretentious philosophy about the unreality, the imaginary nature, of pain breaks down as soon as we subject it to simple tests. So also with the Christian Science attitude towards "drugs," the prescribing of which Mrs. Eddy places in the same category as the denial of God.[8] An obvious comment suggests itself: If drugs cannot cure, it follows that they cannot hurt; will some adherent to this teaching show his consistency in the faith by swallowing a small, but sufficient quantity of oxalic acid? And so, finally, with Mrs. Eddy's singularly futile question, "As power divine is in the healer, why should mortals concern themselves with the chemistry of food?" [9] Without unkindliness, one feels tempted to reply that this kind of language will begin to be convincing when Christian Scientists show their readiness and ability to sustain life on substances chemically certified to be without nutritive properties.

But it is not its denial of physical evil that makes this and allied movements a real menace; dissent as we may from the Christian Science theory of bodily illness, and deplore as we must the fatal results of which we read every now and again when a patient has been persuaded to substitute the Christian Science "healer" for the trained physician—these results concern, to put it rather bluntly, no one but the sufferer and his immediate friends. But when we remarked that the natural man desired to be made well rather than to be made good, we were not merely thinking of one side of Christian Science teaching; we were bearing in mind that the author of *Science and Health* declares the illusoriness of pain only as part of the illusoriness of all evil, moral as well as physical. *Christian Science explicitly denies the reality of sin: and that denial follows with inexorable logic from its first principle—that God is All, and All is Good.* And here rather than in the material domain lies the danger we have to face; this is the side of Mrs. Eddy's doctrine which, the moment it is attractively presented to, and grasped by, half-educated and unstable minds, will, we fear, exercise a fatal fascination over large numbers. For one person who will seriously persuade himself that there is no matter, or that his sore throat is imaginary, there will be a number to welcome the good tidings that what they had hitherto regarded as sin wears in reality no such sinister complexion—that, as Mrs. Eddy openly states, *what seems "vice" is to be explained as "illusions of the physical senses."* That is precisely what every sinner would like to believe. "I have done that, says my memory. I cannot have done that, says my pride, and remains obdurate. In the end, my memory gives in." So wrote Nietzsche, keenly and cynically observant of his kind. As a matter of fact, men would give almost anything to be able to convince themselves that they "have not done that"—not necessarily from pride, but in order to be rid of shame, of remorse, of self-contempt; will not many of them only too eagerly accept this fatal anodyne when it is offered to them in the pretended name of religion?

We have but one comment to urge, one protest to make. It has taken long ages to develop and heighten man's sensitiveness to the distinction between good and evil; we say with the most solemn emphasis that anything calculated to dull that sensitiveness, to wipe out that distinction, to drug the conscience, is nothing less than a crime of high treason against humanity. Better call evil an unfathomable mystery, so long as we also regard it as a dread reality, a foe we must conquer or be conquered by; but to solve the problem by denying its existence, to get over the fact of evil by declaring that all is good—that way not only madness but moral disaster lies. Let us at least understand what this doctrine is, which is being so energetically pressed upon us to-day; and if we see the direction in which that ill-digested pseudo-revelation is likely to lead those who consistently accept it, let us meet this insidious propaganda with equal energy and better arguments. Our first and simplest duty in dealing with the specious doctrine which asserts that evil is "not-being"—a mere illusion which, like the idols spoken of by the Apostle, is "nothing in the world"—is to point out promptly and uncompromisingly that whatever such a reading of the facts may be, and from whatever quarter it may be offered, it is not Christian, but at the furthest remove from Christianity. Shall we be told that "the question is not whether these opinions are dangerous, but whether they are true?" We reply that we are well aware that truth is the highest expediency; but we are not acquainted with any other test of the truth of an opinion save this—whether and how it works. If a speculative theory, when carried into practice, should appear to make straight for pernicious results, in what intelligible sense of the word can it be "true"?

It is the immense merit of Christianity that it has spoken out with no uncertain voice upon this subject; it has never sought to minimise or explain away the fact of moral evil; on the contrary, it has consistently pointed to the true nature of sin, by connecting it vitally and causally with the sacrificial death of the Son of God: *tanta molis erat* (if we may slightly vary the immortal line) *humanam solvere gentem*. A gospel which lightly dismisses this terrible reality, and seeks to hide its hideousness behind a rose-coloured mist of fine words,—such an emasculated gospel is not a message of life, but has the answer of death within itself. That in the past, in a doctrine such as that of man's total depravity, the fact of sin has been over-emphasised, may be readily granted; but in the present all the symptoms indicate that the peril we have to meet is its *under*-emphasis. Against this whole tendency we must resolutely re-assert the Christian standpoint and attitude. Christianity is that religion which affirms in unfaltering accents the reality of evil—but it sets over against it the greater Reality of atoning Love; it proclaims unsparingly the sinfulness and deadliness of sin, but offers us the victory over sin and death through Jesus Christ our Lord.

"*O Timotheus, guard your trust, and eschew the irreverent empty phrases and contradictions of a mis-called 'Science,' professing which some have missed their true aim in regard to the faith.*"

NOTE.

In order to afford an illustration of Christian Science as a thing in being, we reproduce without comment the following report of an inquest, as published in the *Tribune*, on January 9th, 1908:—

Remarkable questions were put by the coroner to witnesses at a Richmond (Surrey) inquest yesterday on Mary Elizabeth Dixon, 58, a Christian Scientist, who died of bronchitis.

Mrs. E. D., of St. John's Road, said that at the request of Mrs. Dixon she gave her Christian Science help—prayer which she had faith would be answered.

The Coroner (Dr. Michael Taylor): Was it?—She was in a state of collapse on Saturday night, but revived much. When Mrs. Dixon had a cold previously it improved wonderfully under Christian Science.

Then Christian Science is effectual if not much is the matter, but is not in the case of a serious illness?—I don't think she wanted to get better.

Is that the way you look at it?—No, I don't. I know God is all-power and ever present.

But if God is all-powerful, as you say, and as we all know, why did you have no response?—I suppose it was my lack of trust in that all-power.

It comes to this, that although He is all-powerful, unless the person praying for another has perfect faith the patient will not recover?—Nothing is impossible to God. The doctor was called in because it was the law.

Then it was too late. It was as much the law to have called him in when the woman was alive. What is the practice with regard to illness?—It is prayer.

If you had a broken leg, would you send for a doctor?—Yes, to set it. I have not sufficient understanding.

Continuing, witness said she did not believe in drugs, but she did in food at present, because her understanding was not sufficient, as she was only a student.

By a Juror: The reason Mrs. Dixon got worse was because of lack of understanding on witness's part.

The Coroner: When she got worse, why did you not send for a doctor?—I asked her if she wanted a doctor to tell me.

Yet she was getting worse owing to your lack of understanding?—I didn't look at it in that light.

B. H., who attended Mrs. Dixon, said she was a trained nurse with nine years' experience. Witness had, during the past two years, become a Christian Scientist nurse. She was not a practitioner.

The Coroner: Has a practitioner any special qualifications?—No, a practitioner is one who prays for another.

The Coroner: Would you give a patient a mustard poultice?—No.

But you would give her a hot-water bottle?—Yes.

Then where do you draw the line? You don't believe in material aid?—No, I believe the other is better.

Do you believe in a judicious continuation of both?—No.

Did you give her beef tea?—Yes, as a nourishment.

But, nurse, you ought to know what every medical man knows, that beef tea is a stimulant. Do you believe in stimulants?—Not at all.

Then why did you give her beef tea?—(After a pause) It was simpler to get.

But it is contrary to your principles. Would you give *sal volatile*?—No.

Witness explained that she called in no other help because she believed prayer was the most effectual.

Why didn't you call in a doctor?—I think the patient should judge for herself.

Even though her brain is clouded and she is dying?—Yes.

On another point the Coroner said: Did our Saviour use food and stimulants?—He gave wine.

Why don't you give wine?—He did not give it in illness, but at a marriage feast.

You want us to believe He gave wine to people who could do without and withheld it from those who wanted it.

Asked a question as to calling in a doctor for surgery purposes, witness said he would only be called in for setting bones and not for an operation.

The Coroner: It amounts to this: you believe the Almighty is a bad surgeon, but a good physician?—Our faith is not yet strong enough.

Dr. Cockell deposed that death was due to acute bronchitis.

Would she have recovered with medical attendance for a week before?—Yes.

The Coroner, in summing up, said there was no doubt Mrs. Dixon was grossly neglected.

The jury returned a verdict of "Death from acute bronchitis, accelerated by gross neglect by Mrs. D. and especially by Nurse H."

The Coroner: I am afraid that will mean manslaughter, which would be too severe. Will you alter it, gentlemen? The jury then altered the verdict to one of "severe censure on Mrs. D. and Miss H. for neglecting to obtain medical aid."

[1] *The Grammar of Assent*, p. 201.

[2] *Rudimental Divine Science*, p. 10.

[3] *Op. cit.*, p. 10. Mrs. Eddy is so incredibly ignorant of the meaning of words in common use that she says, "Mind in matter is pantheism." It has apparently never dawned on her that her own doctrine, "God is All—All is God" is pantheism pure and simple!

[4] *Ibid.*

[5] *Op. cit.*, p. 9.

[6] Dr. Henry Rutgers Marshall, on "Psychotherapeutics," in the *Hibbert Journal*, January, 1909.

[7] The Christian Science healer is supposed to have had his or her powers trained by special tuition, for which, in the ordinary course, a fee is charged. Mrs. Eddy states that she has "never taught a Primary class without several and sometimes seventeen free students in it," but adds significantly "The student who pays must, of necessity, do better than he who does not pay" (*op. cit.*, p. 14). The "necessity" is not quite obvious, but the statement sets one wondering whether it would hold true if for "student" the word "patient" were substituted.

[8] *Op. cit.*, p. 3.

[9] *Ibid.*, p. 13.

CHAPTER IX
DETERMINISM

The under-emphasis of sin, we said, is one of the special dangers which threaten the present age; and nothing is more remarkable or disquieting to observe than the number of attacks that are being made to-day from quarter after quarter, all of them converging upon the same point. Now the cry is raised that sin is a mere mistake, due to ignorance; or that it is merely the absence of something, as a shadow indicates the absence of light[1]; or we are assured that "what we call 'evil' is only incidental to the progress and development of the [universal] order" [2]—a necessary step in evolution. Now again the burden of responsibility is shifted from the shoulders of the individual on to heredity and environment; or compromise with what is known to be moral evil is not only excused as a necessity, but commended as a duty; or the average person's feelings are considerately soothed by the pronouncement that "the mass of a Christian congregation are about as innocent as men and women can well be in a world where natural temptations are so rife, and so many social adjustments discountenance heroic saintliness" [3]—the latter a truly admirable feat of circumlocution. And sometimes, as we have seen, sin and evil are themselves in essence negated—generally in virtue of some pseudo-philosophic or pseudo-scientific "doctrine of a universe"—as when we read that "in a universe . . . there cannot be any room for independent and creative wills, actually thwarting the Good Will." [4] Doubtless, these various statements, whether made in the name of Monism or Determinism, or some form of neo-Christianity, represent a reaction against that over-emphasis which taught that man was by nature under God's wrath and deserving of everlasting torments; but there can be no question that this reaction has gone very far in the direction of the opposite extreme, and that the time has come for reconsideration and a return to more balanced views.

So far as the virtual denial of human freedom, human sin, and indeed of human selfhood, flows from a perversion of the doctrine of Divine immanence, we need not add anything to the observations made in earlier chapters upon this subject; we might, however, quote some pertinent words of Martineau's, affirming and explaining that distinction between the Divine and human personality which can only be ignored to the hopeless confusion of thought:

"The whole external universe, then (external, I mean, to self-conscious beings), we unreservedly surrender to the Indwelling Will, of which it is the organised expression. From no point of its space, from no moment of its time, is His living energy withdrawn, or less intensely present than in any crisis fitly called creative. But the very same principle which establishes a *Unity* of all external causality makes it antithetic to the internal, and establishes a *Duality* between our own and that which is other than ours; so that, were not our personal power known to us as *one*, the cosmical power would not be guaranteed to us as the *other*. Here, therefore, at the boundary of the proper Ego, the absorbing claim of the Supreme will arrests itself, and recognises a ground on which it does not mean to step. Did it still press on and annex this field also, it would simply abolish the very base of its own recognisable existence, and, in making itself all in all, would vanish totally from view. . . . Are we, then, to find Him in the sunshine and the rain, and to miss Him in our thought, our duty and our love? Far from it; He is with us in both: only in the former it is His *immanent* life, in the latter His *transcendent*, with which we are in communion." [5]

Only where this fundamental principle of the non-identity of God and man is recognised, can the facts of human personality, freedom and responsibility for willed acts be rationally based and defended.

At the same time this "otherness" of God, while it is the condition, is not necessarily the guarantee, of our freedom. Determinism is quite compatible, in theory, and has been so found in history, with belief in the Divine transcendence; but it is scarcely compatible with belief in the Divine goodness. There is no *a priori* reason making it inconceivable that the doctrine of absolute predestination might be true; but such a doctrine is not reconcilable with the belief that the Eternal Other is also the Eternal Father. The Divine Autocrat of Calvinism, who pre-ordained some of His creatures to eternal damnation—not for any demerit of theirs, but "just choosing so"—is not unthinkable; what is unthinkable is that we could love such a One—a God who had predestined all human sin and woe, who had fore-ordered things in such a manner that unnumbered hapless souls were doomed evermore to stumble and to suffer. Such a God might inspire a shuddering, wondering, abject awe, but never affection. Only a good God, aiming at the evolution of goodness, the making of character, could have endowed us with freedom, for only through such an endowment can such an aim be realised.

And hence there are perhaps few attitudes so entirely irrational as that which affects to see in a determinist interpretation of man's nature a special reason for optimism. Occasionally one is invited to rejoice in the "great and glorious thought that every man is wholly a product of the Master Workman"; it is even urged that such a conception cannot change our appreciation of what is fine in human thought and action, just as "we do not admire a rose the less because we know that it could no more help being what it is than could a stinging nettle or a fungus." We can only say that such a superficial optimism seems infinitely more open to objection than the temper which, in the face of so much suffering and sin, has to struggle hard sometimes to preserve its faith in the Father's love, and half-wonders if some personal power of evil is not actively engaged in marring God's workmanship. Anyone who can believe that every man, just as he is, represents the Divine intention in concrete form—anyone who can believe this, and glory in the thought—must inhabit a strange world, remote from reality. He can never have learned anything of the greed which condemns myriads of human beings to sunless and degraded lives; he can never have been inside a police-court; he can never have seen hapless womanhood flaunting its be-rouged and be-ribboned shame under the electric light of West End thoroughfares—he can never even have reflected upon any of these things, and rejoiced in the thought that every human being was "wholly the product of the Master Workman." If such a thought does not produce something like despair, it ought to do so; if it does not, then it represents not a conviction but a pose.

As a matter of fact, the determinist creed, with all its professions of charitableness towards the transgressor, and while pretending to soothe us by absolving us from responsibility for wrong-doing, fatally paralyses our endeavours. It is a message, not of liberation from guilt, but of despair. Christianity, even while condemning sin, in its very condemnation speaks of hope; it says to the sinner: "You are guilty—you ought to have done better, and you know it; you are guilty—you ought still to do better, *and you can.*" That is a rousing, vitalising call: the very censure implies the possibility of better things. But Determinism says to the moral wreck: "Not only are you a wreck, but that is all you ever could have been; you not only cannot help being what you are, but in your wretchedness and degradation you are what you could not help being—this was your pre-ordained destiny from the beginning of time. We are not angry with you, any more than we are angry with tigers for being fierce, or with thorns for not bearing grapes; only, being what you are, you never *could* have borne, and never will bear, grapes." Truly a "great and glorious thought"! Determinism makes of the whole world of erring men a hospital, and pronounces every patient an incurable—it is ready to grant kindly, considerate treatment to each, but holds out hopes of recovery to none. Who would not rather submit to a sterner physician, whose ministrations promised to medicine him back to health again! A consistent Determinism, prepared to look stedfastly at things as they are, can, we repeat, lead nowhere but to despair; a conclusion from which determinists, fortunately for themselves, escape by means of the most patent inconsistency.

But we turn to the further contention which we already mentioned in passing, *viz.*, that the acceptance of Determinism would by no means change our admiration of what was fine in human thought and action—just as we did not admire a rose the less because it could not help being fragrant and beautiful. Here we have a very palpable, but all the more significant confusion between things totally different—aesthetics and ethics. Our admiration for a rose is aesthetic; our admiration for goodness is ethical, and we give it with the implicit understanding that the quality we admire is the result of voluntary acts and decisions. All moral judgments imply this; and in practice we know that the experience of moral struggle and moral conquest is intensely real, not to be argued away any more than we can be argued out of any other primary fact of consciousness, which is its own sufficient evidence. Let anyone ask himself quite candidly whether the feeling called forth by some rare work of art resembles remotely the emotion with which he reads of some deed of humble heroism or self-sacrifice; the psychology which discerns here no difference is singularly shallow.

But when the would-be optimistic determinist is shown the sheer fatuity of pretending to rejoice in that everything is just as it is—a singular compliment to the "Master Workman"—he executes a *volte-face* and falls back upon the plea that his doctrine is at any rate a pre-eminently practical one. Instead of vainly deploring imaginary "sins," Determinism would simply have us recognise plain facts: it would arrange for healthy hereditary influences to cradle the coming generations; it would adopt the most enlightened educational, hygienic, reformatory methods; it would provide for all the citizens of the State such an environment as would steadily make for health and beauty and happiness. There are no "sinners," it says, but only the unhappy products of conditions which foster anti-social proclivities as automatically as dirt fosters disease; instead of punishing the products, let us attack the producing conditions, and by sweeping them away bring in the millennium.

Such a plea, it must be admitted, harmonises well with our modern tolerance, our modern zeal for reform; and yet it rests upon a fundamental fallacy. No one, of course, denies the moulding power of heredity and environment; no one denies such an obvious truism as that we cannot expect to grow fine specimens of humanity in the reeking slum or the sweater's workshop. But as environment is a greater power than heredity, so there is only one power greater than environment—and that is our power to alter environment. "But that," protests the determinist, "is just what we hold ought to be done." Certainly; only it is just what, on his presupposition, cannot be done. For if the slum-dweller cannot help being what he is, owing to his environment, neither can the slum-owner, or the legislator, or the community, help being what they are, owing to the self-same cause. In fact, we cannot get the word "ought" from Determinism; it is as much out of place in that connection as a free worker in a slave-compound. But every reform springs from a sense of "oughtness"; and the sense of moral obligation is itself the spontaneous expression of the consciousness of moral freedom. So far as we believe in the duty of reform—or in "duty" itself, *sans phrase*—we have already renounced Determinism, and proclaimed our belief in liberty. Let it be said once more, before we pass from this particular aspect of our subject, that too much may be set down to, or expected from, even environment; everybody knows that from gentle homes, surrounded by what seemed the most favouring influences, there have sprung vicious and depraved characters. We ask ourselves, in encountering such cases, "Wanting is—what?" And the answer must be given in Kant's famous dictum: that which is "the only good thing in the world—*a good will.*"

In one sense, paradoxical as it may sound, much of the strenuous modern advocacy of Determinism or semi-Determinism is a kind of inverted acknowledgment of man's consciousness of freedom, *viz.*, where that consciousness appears as the sense of sin. Of course, when a writer like Mr. Dole assures us that "there is no objection to a moral and spiritual Determinism that binds all things over into the unity of good," [6] we merely reply that on the contrary there is the very serious objection that "all things" are not good. But most advocates of the determinist position are, to do them justice, well aware of the existence of wrong and discord in human life; and their object is, by emphasising the influence of heredity and environment, to remove or at least materially to lighten, the crushing burden of the sense of sin. The same intention underlies the effort, occasionally made, to persuade men that, seeing they are such as God created them, it is not for them to repine at being what they are, nor to "take too serious a view" of any "penchant for revolt"—another delightful phrase—they may discover within themselves; as a recent writer has it, "The responsibility of its presence *and action* does not rest with us, nor are we justified in insulting God who made us, by repenting of what He has done. *We might as well repent of the tiger and the snake, the earthquake and the tempest in nature.*" [7] What are we to say of this attempt to make God answerable, not merely for the presence, but for the action, of whatever impulse to "revolt" of which we may be conscious?

To be quite frank, we cannot think the utterance we have just quoted other than extraordinarily ill-considered. The simple fact that we cannot follow *all* the impulses which arise in us, but have to choose between higher and lower—the fact that we are well aware of this conflict of unharmonisable elements within ourselves, some of which can only triumph at the expense of others—seems sufficiently to dispose of this writer's main contention. We may not be responsible for the presence of these warring instincts, but we are undoubtedly responsible for translating one kind into action while holding the other kind in check. The earthward and the heavenward are in each of us, striving for mastery; but no imagination is vainer than that we can indulge both, or practise the impartiality with which Montaigne's singular devotee lighted one candle to St. George and another to the dragon. If we would realise the type of perfect in the mind, we must not gratify "the penchant for revolt," but exert ourselves to lay—

The ghost of the brute that is walking and haunting us yet and be free;

we must

>   Arise and fly
> The reeling Faun, the sensual feast;
> Move upward, working out the beast,
> And let the ape and tiger die.

Granted that the lower impulses, the inheritance from our animal ancestry, are left in us by Divine decree, they are there, not to be indulged on the plea that to repent would be tantamount to "insulting God who made us," but to be conquered by the exercise of that freedom which is the earnest of our call to claim our birthright as children of God.

But when we are further told that, as well as repent of our actions, we might repent of the tiger and the snake, we are immediately conscious of a double confusion of thought behind that statement; for in the first place, we are not even called upon to repent of *each other's* failings but only of our own, and in the second there is no analogy between ourselves and the tiger and snake, creatures which act according to their animal natures, and are incapable of desiring to be other than they are. Our capacity of, and desire for, better things attest our possession of a measure of liberty, and indicate at once our responsibility for the course we take, and the essential distinction between the animal creation and ourselves—a distinction wittily expressed in the remark that "everybody would admit that very few men are really manly; but nobody would contend that very few whales were really whaley."

But those who seek to spare us the discomfort of repentance by teaching us to declare with a new inflection, "It is He that hath made us, and not we ourselves," forget that there is another side to this argument. It is, of course, very alluring to be told that we are not really blameworthy for acts which hitherto we have blamed ourselves for—that our impulses are God-given—that "the sinner is merely a learner in a lower grade in the school," [8] and so forth; one can understand how grateful is such a morphia injection for deadening the pangs of an accusing conscience. The art of making excuses, as old as the Garden of Eden, will never lack ardent professors or eager disciples. Says Cassius to Brutus:—

> Have you not love enough to bear with me
> When that rash humour which my mother gave me
> Makes me forgetful?

And Brutus answers with a smile:—

> Yes, Cassius, and from henceforth,
> When you are over-earnest with your Brutus,
> He'll think your mother chides, and leave you so!

But, after all, we none of us do exclusively things for which we wish to escape being blamed; there is hardly anyone who could not name some occasion on which he has made some sacrifice, foregone an unfair advantage, declined to listen to selfish promptings, or held some baser impulse in check. None of these things were done for the sake of receiving praise; nevertheless, and quite inevitably, the doer felt praise_worthy_, conscious of an inner accord whose self-attesting power stamped it a reality, and not an illusion. But Determinism leaves no room for this emotion, any more than for that of remorse or blame-worthiness; we cannot get rid of the sense of sin, yet retain the sense of righteousness. The determinist sponge passes over the whole moral vocabulary, not only over the inconvenient parts; it obliterates the terms self-indulgence, dishonesty, cowardice, but the same fate overtakes self-conquest, integrity, bravery. To vary the phrase slightly, we must not, on the determinist hypothesis, insult God by taking credit to ourselves for what He has done. Are we prepared to surrender the approval of our conscience, the new-won self-respect which rewards the successful resistance offered to temptation, as having no basis in fact? And if we are not, what is this but to affirm our freedom and our responsibility alike in doing and forbearing?

And this inner sense of peace or discord, according as we have acted thus or thus—this immediate consciousness that it lay with us to choose aright or amiss—is both anterior and superior to all argument; it asserts itself victoriously against all merely intellectual perplexities, such as are apt to arise when we ask ourselves how man could be free to commit or not to commit an act, in view of the Divine omniscience. The contradiction seems a stubborn one, yet in practice we never feel our freedom circumscribed by it. Probably our difficulty arises largely from the mistake of applying time-relations to God at all, and thinking of eternity as an enormously long period instead of timeless Present, excluding both "unborn To-morrow and dead Yesterday." We, of course, have to think under the category of time, remembering and looking forward; but the Divine *modus cognoscendi* excludes either of these processes, being the timeless act of One who "knoweth altogether"—in whose sight a thousand years are as a day, and a day as a thousand years. To the Eternal Intelligence, living in an unbeginning and unending Present, "past" and "future" must be equally unmeaning; to such a One we cannot but think that all events must be equally and simultaneously present, "for all live unto Him." If we could behold the drama of existence *sub specie aeternitatis*, we might be able to understand how Divine omniscience can co-exist with human freedom; as it is, we can only say, "Such knowledge is too wonderful for us—it is high, and we cannot attain unto it." We know that we cannot know. In any case, even while the Divine omniscience may present itself to us as a necessity of thought, human freedom remains a reality of experience and a postulate of morals.[9]

There are, however, those to whom human freedom presents itself, not as a contradiction to Divine omniscience, but as a contradiction in terms. Man's choice of a course of conduct, they argue, cannot be thought of as other than determined by an efficient cause; but if it is so determined, in what sense can it be free? An uncaused act is strictly speaking unthinkable; but do we not affirm that acts are uncaused when we speak of them as free—in other words, is not the only alternative to Determinism what might be called _in_determinism? The answer is (*a*) that every choice is certainly the result of an efficient cause; but (*b*) the fact of this being so interferes in no wise with the reality of liberty, nor does it contradict the universality of the law of causation. For *the efficient cause is the man himself*, and the fact that he can choose is attested in the very act of choice—which would not be "choice" if there were not at least two real alternatives. We do not quarrel with the obvious truth, stated by Mill, that the will is determined by motives; we contest the assumption that a "free" act is an "uncaused" act. The act is caused or determined by the free choice of a causal self; in strict parlance, indeed, we should have to say that neither acts nor wills, but only human selves, are free. The will is not self-determined, but determined by a self; and this self is able not only to choose between different motives, but to attend to one set of motives to the neglect of others, and even to create motives in order to become able to make a difficult decision.

Let us, however, guard against a possible misconstruction by saying that there is all the difference between this conception of *freedom* and the mere *spontaneity* which is recognised by the followers both of Spinoza and Hegel, a difference which was luminously brought out by Martineau.[10] The Spinozist doctrine of spontaneity, as Mr. Picton points out, means that the individual follows an impulse which "has its antecedents . . . in the chain of invariable sequences." [11] Man, in this view, is "free" to do what he wants, because he wants it; he is *not* free in the sense that he *could* have wanted something different.[12] Nothing could be more frank than Mr. Picton's statements on this point—as when he speaks of the "*free* man's" sense that "all things are of God, and *could not have been otherwise.*"

Of course the obvious retort occurs, (he continues,) that if indeed everything . . . occurs by invariable sequence, all this intellectual gospel of freedom is vain, and exhortations to its acceptance thrown away. And to those who are not satisfied with the freedom of conscious spontaneity, a condition in which we do just as we want to do, though our will is a link in an endless series of untraceable sequences, I suppose this objection must still be final.[13]

The objection is undoubtedly final, because it is absolutely valid; for by freedom we mean the ability to do or leave undone, to act thus or thus, and apart from such an ability moral judgments are quite unthinkable. Where we pronounce praise or blame, the tacit presupposition is always that the object of the pronouncement could have acted differently; and this Spinozism denies.

The same remark applies to the teaching of that modern Absolute Idealism which declares, with Green, that man is his motives, and that he is "free" inasmuch as it is by his own motives that he is governed. It would be as accurate to call an automatic machine "free" on the ground that it is by its own works that it is moved. This is only, as Professor William James aptly calls it, "soft Determinism." If the automaton could decide to slacken or increase its rate of speed, to go or to stop as it liked and where it liked—above all, if it could aim at and devise improvements in its own mechanism so as to make itself a better automaton—it would then be appropriate to speak of it as free; only it would no longer be appropriate to call it an automaton. And similarly it is only if man is able to determine his course of action—if he can "choose" in any real sense, *i.e.*, in the sense that he might choose differently, if he wished to do so—that it can be anything but an abuse of language to speak of him as free; for only in that case can he be an object of approbation or condemnation. If he is merely the sum-total of his motives, he is as little free to act other than he does as a number of chemical elements combined in certain proportions are free to form anything but a definite chemical substance. As Mr. Balfour has well expressed it,[14] "It may seem at first sight plausible to describe a man as free whose behaviour is due to 'himself' alone. But without quarrelling over words, it is, I think, plain that whether it be proper to call him free or not, he at least lacks freedom in the sense in which freedom is necessary in order to constitute responsibility. It is impossible to say of him that he 'ought,' and therefore he 'can,' for at any given moment of his life his next action is by hypothesis strictly determined." But the freedom of which we are conscious—*e.g.*, in every experience of conflict between inclination and duty—is something altogether different; we know that we can yield or resist, choose between, reinforce, and if necessary *make*, our motives.[15]

But is not sin, it is sometimes asked, inevitable *per se*, and in that sense natural to man, and if so, how can we be blamed for what we could not avoid? And again, is there not some truth in the statement that much that we call evil has been incidental to the progress of the race, just as the discords produced by the learner on a musical instrument are necessary incidents in the process which will teach him by and by to charm the ear with the perfect harmony? Such questions are frequently put forward; let us see if we are able to clear away the misunderstandings to which they bear witness.

(1) Admitting that a free moral being must be able in theory to choose the wrong as well as the right, it should in the first place be observed that the possibility of that or any course does not render it *inevitable* for him to take it, and it is only the possibility that is given. But it may be justly argued that since as a matter of fact all men sin, we cannot pretend that we are merely dealing with a theoretical possibility, but must pronounce sin to be *de facto* natural to man as well as inevitable—for who has ever avoided it? Let us observe what follows: this, and no more, that sin is "natural" only in the sense in which disease is "natural"—*viz.*, as a disorder to which the human frame may become subject, but nevertheless a disorder. As physical disease entails a diminution of physical life, so sin entails a diminution of our moral and spiritual life, an alienation of the soul from God; and while anyone may thus choose to describe sin—the wilful misuse of faculties lent us for other ends—as natural, it is significant that the result of sin is quite _un_natural, *viz.*, a state of disunion between the soul and God. So much is this the case that the aim of all religion is to bring about a cessation of this unhappy state, and to effect the healing of the discord created by man's transgression. True religion treats sin, not as an error to be explained away, but as a wall of partition to be broken down; the essential aim of religion is atonement, man's reconciliation to God.

(2) But it is further urged that in historical retrospect, and in the light of evolution, it is difficult to avoid the conclusion that in the course of man's development from a savage and barbaric condition all manner of ills—bloodshed, slavery, etc.—have been necessary stages; may not, then, sin be claimed as constituting part of the Divine plan? And if such was the case once, may it not be the case still? Here we are dealing with a very obvious confusion; for while man is in a low and undeveloped state, a good many acts which would be sins if committed by people on a higher level, have not that character at all. It is quite impossible, *e.g.*, to read the Homeric poems and find in them any trace or indication that deceit, war and massacres are regarded with so much as moral distaste; the men of the Homeric age had

simply not risen to that moral height, and it would be futile to judge them by the standards of a more advanced civilisation. Undoubtedly, in its slow evolution from sub-human origins, the race passes through long sub-moral stages during which the animal instincts—"moods of tiger or of ape"—are still in the ascendant; it is only gradually that man becomes aware of certain practices with shame, disgust or remorse, and it is only then that we can begin to speak of the indulgence of the passions which prompt those practices as "sin." When Paul calls the law the strength of sin, or says that the law came in that the trespass might abound, he states a truth, but sees it, if one may say so, out of focus; for the law was not arbitrarily imposed in order to brand a multitude of harmless acts as offences, but in proportion as the moral law is discerned by man's mind, acts which formerly were merely non-moral begin to range themselves on this side or that, as right and wrong. True, even when our moral perceptions have thus been quickened, we shall not always "rule our province of the brute" with a strong hand—true also that, owing to our earthly nature, "in many things we all stumble;" but so far from viewing these failures complacently, they ought to spur us to more earnest endeavours to leave our lower inheritance behind. The truth concerning the "inevitableness" of sin was stated by our Lord when He said, "It must needs be that occasions"—*viz.*, of stumbling—"come; but woe to that man through whom the occasion cometh." Sin as such, as an "occasion," is inevitable; but for any particular sin, for acting contrarily to the known best, the individual is responsible— and greatest of all is the responsibility of one who knowingly and of design becomes an "occasion of stumbling" to another, making sin more difficult to avoid, or positively inciting another to wrong-doing. We do not forget the inequalities of moral endowment, nor do we leave out of sight that a temptation which for one man scarcely so much as exists may prove well-nigh irresistible to another; but the judgment upon each is in the wise and Fatherly hands of Him who knoweth our frame, and remembereth that we are dust.

We have seen that Determinism, in spite of its humanitarian and even optimistic pretensions, when it is consistently applied falsifies every one of its promises; it is worth while to ask ourselves yet once more what is likely to be the effect of this doctrine upon the characters of those who seriously entertain it. Mill, in his frigid and precise, yet scrupulously just manner, expressed the opinion that

The free-will doctrine, by keeping in view precisely that portion of the truth which the word necessity puts out of sight, namely the power of the mind to co-operate in the formation of its own character, has given to its adherents a practical feeling much nearer to the truth than has generally (I believe) existed in the minds of necessarians. The latter may have had a stronger sense of the importance of what human beings can do as to shape the characters of one another; but the free-will doctrine has, I believe, fostered in its supporters a much stronger spirit of self-culture.[16]

If for "self-culture" we substituted self-reliance, buoyancy, a sense of responsibility, we should scarcely go too far; for, indeed, it would be difficult to say from what sources the consistent determinist is to derive these qualities. He regards himself as the inevitable product of forces which have moulded him into that particular shape and no other; he cannot help himself or change his character by one hair's-breadth; he views his own life, as has been well said, not in the light of a story which he can carry on as he may choose, but as a sum which must finish in a given way; and his one dismal consolation is that he is not responsible for his shortcomings. He can but say with his favourite sage:—

> The Ball no question makes of Ayes and Noes,
> But Here or There as strikes the Player goes;
>   And He that toss'd you down into the Field,
> He knows about it all—*He* knows—HE knows!

But to believe that no effort can avail will certainly not inspire anyone to make such an effort; on the contrary, the likelihood is only too great that such a belief will upon occasion serve as a welcome excuse for not making it. It has been said that Determinism, if not a very heroic creed, will at any rate make for tolerance and charity towards human failings; but nothing is more certain than that this kind of charity will, in practice, begin—while its tendency will be also to end—at home.

This estimate, it is true, is often warmly challenged; in actual life, we are told, many of those who profess determinist principles are notorious for their strenuous moral calibre, and certainly not open to the charge of laxity. Let that statement be ungrudgingly accepted; what it proves is no more than that prussic acid is entirely harmless—provided it is not taken. We are quite willing to admit that Determinism, provided it is not put into practice, is nothing more than a mistaken theory. So long as men are content to be determinists in their studies and libertarians everywhere else, no particular mischief is likely to ensue; and it is matter of common experience, and for much congratulation, that our theoretical determinists should so far obey the instinct of moral self-preservation as to be for the most part practical libertarians, freely pronouncing praise and blame on human conduct, and feeling praise- and blameworthy themselves. But if they were logical and consistent determinists, they would do and feel no such thing; for the praise we give to a well-poised spring-cart is one thing, and the praise we give to a well-poised character is another. And again, given a man who really believed, or whom it suited to believe, that he was quite irresponsible for his actions, and that no morally valid censure could attach to him for gratifying some appetite or passion, one cannot help suspecting that the result would be something much worse than mere laxity. That most persons who argue in favour of Determinism do not act up to its principles, is surely nothing in the doctrine's recommendation; on the other hand there is always the unpleasant possibility that some day they may begin to take their philosophy seriously. And just as one would not like prussic acid to lie about promiscuously where all and sundry could have access to it, lest there should be a great deal of accidental poisoning, so we are justified in viewing the broadcast dissemination of determinist theory not merely with the antipathy one may feel towards intellectual error, but with the apprehension excited by a moral danger. Every system or movement which involves the denial of evil or of freedom—the denial or under-emphasis of sin—menaces not only religion in the narrower sense, but the structure of civilisation itself.

The rock upon which all these theories make shipwreck is the fact that we cannot abolish the reality of sin and leave the reality of goodness intact. Saint and sinner, hero and coward, martyr and traitor, all, as we have seen, are reduced by Determinism to a common level where there is neither admiration nor censure, but at most a vague wonder at all the unnecessary suffering—for *that* at any rate remains real—involved in this profoundly futile procession of phenomena; and that is a conclusion to which humanity has always refused, and will always refuse, to reconcile itself. If we wish to see how utterly a deterministic conception empties morality of meaning, we need only turn to the earthly career of our Lord, and ask ourselves what it is that gives to that life and death their poignant significance but the voluntariness with which the Saviour took each successive step on the road from His native Nazareth to the place called Calvary. Think of Him simply as the product of a compelling Force, unable to act otherwise than He did, and at one stroke all that moved us to gratitude, to admiration, all that appealed to us most deeply, is gone. There can be no such thing as compulsory heroism or non-voluntary self-sacrifice; moral judgments upon "inevitable" conduct are merely absurd—we do not bestow moral approval upon this kind of higher automatism.

Sometimes, indeed, in a connection like this, an attempt is made at some sort of compromise: granted, it is said, that each separate action of Christ's was voluntary, yet His life-purpose as a whole was surely pre-determined, and not left to Him to adopt or refuse. Yet how impossible, upon closer reflection, is this species of semi-Determinism! Every single act of Jesus was voluntary; but His whole life and character and purpose—which is just the sum-total of these single, voluntary acts—these, we are to believe, were strictly necessitated. He could choose every step of a way which was yet absolutely chosen for Him, so that He could tread no other! A tremendous decision like His going to Jerusalem lay within His power; but the aim and meaning of His life, viewed as a whole, He had no power of voluntarily determining. That, to our mind, is a wholly irrational position; one might as reasonably say, "Every link of this chain is golden; but the chain itself is iron." Simple consistency requires the admission that if the chain is iron, so must the links be, and if the links are golden, so must be the chain.

We say again—all that enshrines Jesus in our hearts, all that gives its redemptive power to His love-prompted death, and its significance to Calvary, rests upon the fact of His moral freedom. He had *power* to lay down His life; therein lay the glory of His self-surrender. He was, indeed, God's instrument in effecting the reconciliation of sinners to the Divine Love, but it rested with Him to decide whether He would be that instrument or no, and the course He chose was not that of mechanical necessity, nor was the decision to which He came a following in the line of least resistance. In accepting the pain and shame of the Cross, Jesus worked His Father's will; but that will was not imposed upon Him from without, but freely responded to from within. As the author of the *Theologia Germanica* has it, a man should strive "to be to the Eternal Goodness what his hand is to a man": but all the ultimate splendour of the achievement is bound up with the initial possibility of the striving. Not only the yearning love of God, but the conquering freedom of Man is finally attested by that blood-red seal which bears the impression of a Cross.

[1] So *e.g.*, *In The Theology of Civilisation*, by Charles F. Dole, p. 49.

[2] *The Coming People*, by the same author, p. 49.

[3] *The Over-Emphasis of Sin*, by the Rev. Alexander Brown, in the *Hibbert Journal*, April, 1909, p. 616.

[4] *The Theology of Civilisation*, p. 61. It would, of course, have been easy to give references from other authors; but there is an extraordinary family-likeness between the writers of this School, extending down to the very phrasing of their ideas.

[5] *A Study of Religion*, vol. ii., pp. 166, 179.

[6] *Theology of Civilisation*, p. 129.

[7] The Rev. Alexander Brown, *loc. cit.*, p. 619; italics ours.

[8] Dole, *op. cit.*, p. 101.

[9] The analogy of the tyro and the expert chess-player—the tyro "free," yet the expert foreseeing and holding the issue of the game in his own hands—is only superficially plausible. There seems, however, one other possible

explanatory hypothesis, though it is here advanced only in the most tentative manner: may it not be possible for the Most High to impose a limitation upon His infinite knowledge corresponding to that self-limitation of His infinite power which we regard as a necessary assumption? It would be difficult on *a priori* grounds to declare such a thing to be inconceivable. When Paul spoke of himself as "determined not to know anything save Jesus Christ," he signified his intention of shutting out from his knowledge whole ranges of facts, for reasons dictated by the purpose he had in hand; and as a matter of every-day experience, we all practise something like this habitually, voluntarily narrowing the range of our consciousness and our immediate interests for one cause and another. Might not God, if the reality of our freedom could not be guaranteed in any other way, and if that freedom was necessary for the attainment of His purpose with man, forbear in some measure, however slight, to exercise His omniscience? We are well aware that the subject admits of nothing more than reverent surmise; and having stated our suggestion, we simply leave it with the reader as one of those possibilities which will appeal differently to different minds.

[10] *Types of Ethical Theory*, vol. ii., pp. 31 ff.

[11] *Spinoza*, p. 195.

[12] Cp. *Pantheism*, p. 74.

[13] *Spinoza*, p. 196.

[14] In *Mind*, October, 1893; quoted in Professor Upton's invaluable Hibbert Lectures on *The Bases of Religious Belief*, p. 293, n.

[15] It may be interesting to quote a recent popular statement of the neo-Hegelian position in regard to this question: "The feeling that we are free is true in this sense, that the cause of a moral deed is a motive within us, and not some power outside us. But this motive moves us because of what we are, because of our characters, and the character is the product of inherited instincts, appetites and passions, modified by controlling ideas which have been acquired since our birth. Mr. Blatchford is so far right in his book, *Not Guilty*. The inward and outward conditions of a man's life, of course, *make him what he is inevitably*. We choose, but our choice is governed by all our past, and by present circumstances. . . We have our ancestors rolled up in us. A man is the last result of the universe. All is law. All is inevitable by the laws of life:" (The Rev. G. T. Sadler, B.A., LL.B., in the *Clarion*, June 11th, 1909). That, of course, is not liberty at all; and the logical honours appear to rest with Mr. Blatchford, who, arguing on the same assumptions, declares sin to be a meaningless term, seeing that "man is not responsible for his nature, nor for the acts prompted by that nature."

[16] *System of Logic*, vol. ii., p. 412 (third edition).

CHAPTER X
MORALITY AS A RELIGION

That minimising or denial of moral evil with which we dealt in the preceding pages, is common to, and follows as the corollary from, all systems in which the personality and transcendence of God are either explicitly denied or virtually ignored. Monism, that is to say,—whether of the idealistic or the materialistic variety, whether pantheist or atheist in complexion—finds its ethical counterpart in Determinism.

There are, however, in our pathetically restless age a number—probably a growing number—of serious men and women who attack the problem from the opposite end. Weary of speculation, and leaning on the whole to the side of negation rather than affirmation in matters of theology, they say that one thing at any rate is left, a certainty of which no one can deprive them, an ideal sufficient to inspire mankind—the supreme worthiness of the good life. While the creeds of the Churches divide their respective adherents from each other, here, they tell us, is a basis upon which all can unite, and which therefore should assuredly prove adequate and attractive; nay, since religion is valued for the kind of life it produces—since the tree is judged neither by its name, nor age, nor foliage, but simply and solely by its fruit—shall we not say that morality itself is the true and only religion, that residuum of valid and vital truth which remains when all the errors of supernaturalism have been purged and filtered away? Certainly there are those in our own day who, while definitely rejecting the sanctions and authority of religion in its commonly accepted meaning, are fully convinced that to live an unselfish life is a duty incumbent on man, and who honestly endeavour to practise what they believe. That being so, is not faith shown to be practically superfluous, and the autonomy and sufficiency of ethics a demonstrated fact?

Such, in short, is the contention of the Ethical Movement, so ably and often eloquently represented by leaders like Felix Adler, W. M. Salter, Washington Sullivan, Stanton Coit, and others; all these teachers with one accord deprecate and dismiss theological doctrines as at best not proven, at worst a hindrance, and commend instead morality as the all-embracing, all-sufficing and all-saving religion. To quote Mr. Salter, who certainly speaks with authority for his side:—

A religion that will teach us how to live, that will hold up clear and high the laws of life and win us to obedience to them—this is the religion the world needs, and it is the only true religion; all others, all that seek to make something else sacred, that make men put their trust in "God" or Christ or the Virgin or the Bible or the Church or its sacraments and rites, are a diverting of man from the real issue; they are the blind leading of the blind; they are a delusion and a snare.[1]

Mr. Salter is, indeed, willing to show "charity" for the belief "that the authority of the right is in some way connected with God"; but it is the charity that may be extended to an exploded superstition on account of certain beneficent associations that cling to it. "If by the term 'God,'" he says,[2] "was meant simply the reason and nature of things, it might perhaps be freely used; but the word means something else to most persons"—and therefore the honest ethicist will not employ it. For this sensible and candid course we cannot but feel thankful; Mr. Salter at any rate knows well enough that there is all the difference between "the reason and nature of things"—between a mere "totality of being"—and a personal God.

We cannot disguise from ourselves that the present juncture is in many respects singularly favourable to the ethical movement; to not a few who have lost their earlier faith and feel the need of something to take its place, Ethicism will seem to meet that want, and they will accordingly give a wistful, grateful hearing to what Mr. Salter and his colleagues have to preach. Probably, indeed, it will be people of a higher than the average intellectual and moral calibre who will seek to fill the void left by Agnosticism by embracing "morality as a religion"; and more particularly is this likely to happen when this cult has for its apostles, men of high character and gracious personality. It is for that very reason that we are bound to examine this plea carefully, and to ask ourselves whether it is really possible, as we are assured, "by purely natural and human means to help men to love, know, and do the right." [3] The issue is no less than a momentous one; for if religion, as generally understood, is a mere graceful superfluity when it is not "a delusion and a snare," very vast changes are bound to follow the recognition of such a fact. Dr. Coit may be a little premature in making his voluminous arrangements for the adaptation of the Established Church and the Book of Common Prayer to the uses of ethical religion; but if ethicists can convince us of the validity of their claims, then we must look forward to the fruitful service of man taking the place of the fruitless service of God.

Now the first remark we have to make is that as a matter of fact and of history a high morality has never made its appearance apart from religion. Such as they are, our moral code and moral standards at their best are the product of the Christian faith; the ethical movement has neither evolved a morality of its own, nor has it anything better to put in the place of that which we owe to Christianity. Such suggestions of alleged defects in the ethics of the Gospel as are brought forward by Mr. Salter—*e.g.*, that Jesus lacked "a scientific sense of cause and effect"; that He failed to inculcate "intellectual scrupulousness and honesty"; that we cannot go to Him for "political conceptions" and "industrial ethics," and so forth—strike one as palpably trivial, irrelevant, and made to order;[4] and leaving these not very imposing criticisms on one side, it is simply a fact that the highest laws of life were declared by Jesus Christ, and have never been superseded. And since ethicists have nothing better to propose in the domain of conduct than what we find in the Gospel—since the "higher law," as formulated by Mr. Salter, reduces itself to altruism versus living for self—there is nothing harsh in saying that the ethical movement proposes merely to take over Christian morality minus its Christian setting. If a simile may be allowed, we should say that this new firm has no goods of its own manufacture; it intends to trade with the stock, and hopes to take over the goodwill, of the old. Whether that is a feasible *modus operandi* is another question, at which we shall glance presently; for the moment we would simply insist upon the fact that hitherto at any rate the ultimate sanction of morality has always been the *religious* sanction. The Churches, in basing morality on religion, can at any rate point to some actual achievements in the past; on the other hand those who maintain that morality is independent of religious belief, and that human conduct will actually rise to a higher level when this truth is recognised, must pardon us if we tell them that they are merely issuing promissory notes which may or may not be honoured when they fall due. A certain extremely important thing has been done—we will not say perfectly, but nevertheless done—in a certain way and by certain means for a very long time; anyone who assures us that he will accomplish the same important thing for us without the means which we have hitherto deemed indispensable, can hardly be surprised if we reply that while we do not doubt his entire good faith, we cannot possibly content ourselves with his bare promises in so vital a matter.

But when we say this, we shall at once be met with the rejoinder that it is manifestly unfair to argue as if Ethicism were all promise and no performance. Are there not plenty of kindly, conscientious, well-conducted agnostics who might serve as models to some of their Church-going neighbours? And have we not already referred to some of the ethical teachers themselves as men of high character and gracious personality? All this may be very readily admitted; but all this has not an atom of bearing upon the matter in hand. The question really is not whether certain avowed agnostics are not as good men as certain professing Christians; but whether the moral excellences of the good agnostic are the *product*, the fruit, of agnosticism, in the same sense in which the virtues of the Christian are the *product* of Christianity. The answer to that question must be unhesitatingly in the negative. There is no disputing the historical fact that the force which has been most potent in building up our Western civilisation is none other than Christianity; the ethics which have shaped and guided right conduct through all these centuries are Christian ethics. Think as we will about dogma, few will feel competent to contest Lecky's verdict, when the historian of Rationalism and of European Morals declares that Christianity "has been the main source of moral development in Europe"; we know what this religion has done, because its actual record is open to inspection. To quote Lecky again, "Christianity has produced more heroic actions and formed more upright men than any other creed." Now Agnosticism has not created its own moral system; agnostic morality at its highest has so far grown in Christian soil, and to say that the flower will continue to grow in quite a different soil is to make a very bold and very hazardous prophecy. In the West we have never had anything like an agnostic civilisation, which would allow us to test the effects of non-belief upon conduct on a large scale; in the East, it is true, Japan offers us something like an agnostic civilisation, but those who are best acquainted with that nation are least inclined to exalt her performances in the domain of ethics. Japanese commercial morality is notoriously low; while Japan's dealings with Korea have called forth the unmeasured denunciations of European eyewitnesses. The material advances and military exploits of this virtually agnostic nation must not blind us to other and less admirable features; it would, indeed, seem that this highly-gifted race, while frantically eager to "gain the whole world," has not yet discovered its own soul, and the familiar question, "What shall it profit?" inevitably suggests itself.

But not only has Agnosticism so far not grown its own morality; there is yet another consideration which leads us to listen with a certain measure of scepticism to the assurances of those who say that right conduct will survive though religion be surrendered. It has perhaps not been generally observed that just as the virtuous agnostic is generally the child of Christian parents, so by a seeming irony he is often found to be the father of Christian children: there is hardly a genuine case on record where "free-thought," Agnosticism, Rationalism, has descended from parents to children to the third or fourth generation without a break, and the practical non-existence of such cases proves something of real and great importance. It has been said that pure-bred Londoners die out in three generations at most, unless new blood from the country is brought in to replenish their failing vital power. If unbelief shows the same incapacity to propagate itself by natural descent—if the descendants of unbelievers show a marked tendency to "revert to type," *i.e.*, to religion—such a fact suggests only one adequate explanation, *viz.*, the instinct of self-preservation, a return to the soil which made the growth of the flower possible. The virtues of the agnostic may be not unfairly compared to cut flowers, which may continue to shed their perfume for awhile, but are bound to fade before long. Our agnostic ethicists, being themselves the products of a Christian civilisation, may commend, approve and practise—they may *wear* the Christian virtues; that those virtues will bear transplanting into an agnostic soil and flourish in an agnostic climate is a highly dubious proposition. We can only say that available experience seems to be against it. The Christian morality implies the Christian religion which has created it; as for the high-minded, altruistic individual agnostic, he must simply be pronounced a credit to Christianity.

We say "the high-minded *individual* agnostic," because candour compels us to go on to state that generally speaking those who have thrown religion to the winds hardly strike one as standing on a particularly high ethical level. One can only go by facts; and the facts are that the frequenters of the betting-ring, the dram-shop, the light-minded, pleasure-seeking throng that flutters from amusement to amusement without any interest in life's serious duties—these are hardly drawn from the Church-going strata of society. Religion says "no" to this whole mode of life; and unbelief is most frequently, and in its most typical forms, found where the restraints of religion have proved too irksome to be tolerated. Before arguing in the abstract that morality is independent of religion, and will be advanced by its abandonment, it would perhaps be better to observe the average, concrete case of the man who has cut himself adrift from religious beliefs and influences; then it will be time to decide whether we should like to see the experiment tried on a national scale. It is easy to theorise *in vacuo*; in practice we are well aware that without the sanctions and the guardianship of religion morality tends to sink to the level where the accepted motto is the hedonist's "Let us eat and drink and be merry, for to-morrow we die."

But at this point another objection will be raised; "surely," it is said, "we do not seriously maintain that men are kind to their families, honest in their every-day transactions, truthful in speech, and so forth, merely because they believe that to do so is to act in accordance with Divine injunction, and that if this belief were suddenly destroyed we should be reduced to moral chaos." But this argument, so frequently met with in this connection, misapprehends the real issue. We do not dispute that the elements of moral conduct begin to be inculcated wherever there is any social life at all. Where there is any living together, complete selfishness is impossible; there must come into being a rough law of give-and-take, a recognition of mutual rights to be respected, a certain loyalty from the individual towards the tribe, which in turn befriends and defends each of its members. Quite a number of rudimentary virtues are thus developed by the force of public opinion, which cannot tolerate flagrantly anti-social acts from one member of the community towards the rest; murder, violence, theft, false witness—these and the like offences are suppressed with a strong hand, without the need of a special supernatural revelation to decree "Thou shalt not." To be brief, there is no doubt that this social pressure is powerful enough to insist upon behaviour which will regulate most of the ordinary relationships of life in a fairly satisfactory manner—*i.e.*, relationships between equals or members of the same community. The latter is a highly important qualification; where purely natural sanctions obtain, equal rights might be enjoyed by all *bona fide* members of the tribe, but the same rights would not necessarily extend to an alien. And even within the community governed by such sanctions the weaker, and especially the weakest, did not rank as equals; among the most highly civilised nations of antiquity, the Greeks and Romans, infanticide and exposure flourished—indeed, as Lecky points out,[5] by the ideal legislations of Plato and Aristotle, and by the actual legislations of Lycurgus and Solon, infanticide was positively enjoined. Nothing can be more significant than to find in the *Self-Tormentor* of Terence the very character who expresses the noble sentiment, "I am a man, and deem nothing that is human alien from me," giving instructions that if the child that is to be born to him should be a girl, it is to be put to death. The public opinion of an enlightened and cultured paganism countenanced such deeds without reproach; it was Christianity, or rather He who said, "Suffer the little children to come unto Me," that put a stop to these barbarities.

The point which we wish to establish is this: that while "evolutional ethics" and natural sanctions will carry us a certain way, they will certainly not carry us all the way; indeed, the moment we come to the higher reaches of character, these sanctions are seen to be quite inadequate. Why, *e.g.*, should the conviction be born in man, and become a governing conviction, that he must under no circumstances commit a certain act, though to do so would be easy and advantageous, and detection not to be feared? Why should the moral consciousness of the higher races accept the principle which places self-sacrifice above self-seeking? There is only one explanation for this paradoxical phenomenon: it is that, as men rise in the moral scale, there dawns on them the sense of a law that is not of this world, an *Ought-to-be*, which speaks with a strange authority, and will not be denied; and when this authority is properly interpreted, it reveals a Righteous and Sovereign Will to which we owe unconditional obedience.

And here we may quote in support some significant words of Mr. Salter's— words whose full significance, we venture to think, that able and distinguished writer hardly realised when he penned them: "*The whole meaning of ethics is in the sense of an invisible authority; to bow to custom, to public opinion or to law, is moral idolatry.*" [6] "Whatever else I may doubt about, I cannot doubt the law of duty—that there is a right and a wrong; that the right obliges me, that I ought to do it. . . . The law is over all, though it were never obeyed. . . . Ethics is nothing but the response which man and man make to the higher order of things. . . . Ecstasy is the grace heaven sets upon the moment in which the soul weds itself to the perfect good." [7] Let us see what is implied in these truly remarkable statements. The real sanctions of moral conduct are not the sanctions of expediency or force, but are derived from a higher law, an invisible authority; the finest morality is man's free response to a higher order. But, we ask, what is this higher order, this note of command, but the expression of a higher Will? And how can there be a higher Will without a Higher Personality, a God who impresses His law upon us and makes us aspire after the ideal good? Mr. Salter explicitly denies that the moral virtues come "from below, from prudence, from the sense of decency, from longsighted selfishness; they who think so," he declares, in a fine burst, "never breathed the climate of morality." [8] But if not from below, they must come from above; and this "above" really must be something more than an atmospheric conception. Will Mr. Salter help us to determine its nature more clearly? He says, "The Mighty Power, hid from our gaze by the thin screen of nature and of nature's laws . . . is with our struggles after a perfect right" [9]; *but if this Mighty Power*, which is not so much expressed as hidden by nature's laws—which therefore transcends nature—*is in the highest sense moral, how can it be less than personal?* It is this Power which, according to our author, gives us the vision of the ideal, this Power which sets the mark of its approval upon our surrender to its behests, this Power which manifests its character in doing justice upon individuals and nations alike, weeding out the selfish, the wanton, the luxurious, and preserving the pure and upright; may we not ask what reason there is for withholding from that Power the one adequate name of God?[10]

Let us pursue and emphasise this thought a little further. Already we have seen that—*teste* Mr. Salter—the highest ethics require our belief in a mighty, transcendent and benevolent Power; that admission means nothing less than the surrender of naturalism in morals—it is an acknowledgment that ultimately a true ethic involves and presupposes a metaphysic. Indeed, when Mr. Salter speaks of ethical religion, the same implication is there. Religion signifies a living and personal relationship between the worshipper and the object of his worship: we can stand in such a relationship to a living, personal God, in harmony with whose will alone we are able to find our true happiness; we cannot stand in such a relationship to an impersonal power or a universal order. Mr. Salter speaks of man "bending hushed and subdued, as he thinks of those mighty laws on which the health and safety of the race depends," and calls that a religion; we submit that so far as such an emotion is religious, it means that behind those mighty laws there stands a mighty Lawgiver, whom we worship and seek to obey because He is good. We can keep a law, we can conform to it so as to escape hurt, but we cannot worship it except when we conceive of it as the manifestation of a good Will; neither can we derive moral stimulus from an abstract ideal. It is when the ideal speaks in us and to us as the behest of the Living God—above all, when it stands before us incarnated, made actual in the Son of God—that it becomes dynamic, drawing and uplifting and transforming men into the Divine likeness. We are not greatly helped by such a statement as that the bare idea of morality, quite apart from faith in God, "may be the supreme passion to a man"; we have to deal with things as they are, and in actual life we well know that the most commonplace presentation of the Gospel has been more of a force in the making of character and as an inspiration to righteousness than the most refined philosophical Ethicism.

And now let us show, from yet another point of view, as we think may be done quite simply and cogently, that it is impossible rationally to get away from the theistic position if we are in earnest about morality, viewed as the pursuit of the ideal. In order to engage in such a pursuit, we must in the first place be free agents, able to choose between conflicting motives and to follow the right. If our actions are necessitated, then to speak of our "pursuing" this or that course, choosing and rejecting, is of course a mere contradiction in terms. But if the universe, including ourselves, is simply the resultant outcome of the interaction of unconscious mechanical forces, freewill is an absolute illusion, and Determinism the only true theory; and again, if Determinism is true, we cannot choose, we cannot strive—in a word, we cannot help being what we are. Hence, if morality in any intelligible sense is to exist at all, we must be free; and only a personal and transcendent God could have conferred on us the faculty of freewill.

We pass on to one or two final considerations. One of our ethicists, who genially informs us that "theology is discredited . . . and the world is indifferent to what the Church either thinks or says," writes as follows: "The Ethical Movement believes that the good life has an imperative claim upon us because of its supreme worth for humanity." [11] As against this statement we have no hesitation in affirming that only religion, in the accepted sense of the term, can give us the absolute conviction of the absolute supremacy of moral claims—the assurance that it were better to suffer, to hunger, to be despised and rejected of men, to die on a cross, than to violate one of these. Grant that the good life is of supreme worth for humanity; yet supposing a man is sorely tempted to obtain some immense advantage or to gratify some consuming passion, at the cost of injuring someone else—suppose he can do so with safety and success—why should he prefer humanity's interests to his own? Why, indeed? We make bold to say that no one in the throes of conflict between duty and desire, at the moment of moral crisis, has ever been influenced by the worth of his action for humanity. The ultimate sanction of right conduct must be drawn from a Source beyond humanity, which enjoins the right at all costs—from Him who is humanity's Maker and Ruler.

And the same fact is borne witness to by the experience which waits upon wilful wrong-doing, by the sense of sin. Such an emotion can never be inspired by an impersonal order with which we have come into conflict, but only by a personal Will against which we are conscious of having offended. The man who disregards the law of gravitation and falls from a ladder, experiences one kind of painful sensation; but the man who disregards the law of righteousness and falls into sin, experiences quite a different kind of painful sensation—the sensation, not of self-pity, but of self-accusation and remorse, because it is God's holiness against which he has transgressed; and that feeling finds utterance age after age in the agonised cry, "Against Thee, Thee only, have I sinned, and done that which is evil in Thy sight."

The truth is, those who claim to set up morality as a religion, while declaring "the personal Deity of theology illusory," are engaged in an impossible task; and it is because of the inherent hopelessness of their enterprise that we must raise our voice in warning to any who may be tempted to put faith in their fair promises. The ethicist's intentions are admirable; but he sets about their realisation in a manner which dooms him and them to failure. Let us have practice without theory, he says, the superstructure without the foundation, the fruit without the root, works without the faith which produces works: and such being the nature of his undertaking, he fares accordingly, a spectacle of ineffectual goodness, wondering why the world declines to listen to his so reasonable gospel. But the world continues to cling to an ultra-rational Gospel because it is instinctively aware that morality rests upon ultra-rational sanctions. Ethicism may borrow from Christianity the doctrine of the brotherhood of man, but it has no explanation to give of the basis supporting that axiom—why we ought to regard each human being as having certain indefeasible claims upon us, so that we may not treat him as a mere means subserving our ends. That position can never be defended on purely natural grounds; in the last analysis the brotherhood of man has a right to be accepted as true only by those who believe in the Fatherhood of God.

In conclusion, as all true morality pre-supposes religion, so it is only religion which can supply the strongest incentive and encouragement to the good life; for it is religion alone which has the promise that the Good shall and must prevail, that the stars in their courses are fighting on the side of right and truth, and that it shall be well or ill with us according as we range ourselves on that side or in opposition to it. Take away the idea of a God whose will is that righteousness shall triumph, that life shall be lord of death, and love victorious over all, and we have no guarantee but that all the efforts and sacrifices of martyr and reformer may be in vain, and the hope of the world a delusion. It is only the believer who can never despair, who knows that his work will endure and enrich the world—that there will be no collapse or final disarray, that the world is no blot nor blank, but means intensely and means good. It is that faith which makes endeavour and surrender worth while; that faith—the assurance of things hoped for, the evidence of things not seen—which alone gives us a right to sing Felix Adler's noble hymn:—

> And the work that we have builded,
>   Oft with bleeding hands and tears,
> Oft in error, oft in anguish,
>   Will not perish with our years,
> It will rise and shine transfigured
>   In the final reign of light;
> It will pass into the splendours
>   Of the City of the Light.

For the assurance which breathes in these lines rests on a previous, deeper assurance: it is that which the Christian expresses in the words, "*If God be for us, who is against us?*"

[1] *Ethical Religion*, p. 48.

[2] *Ibid*, p. 39.

[3] See *A Few Points about Ethical Societies*, a tract issued by the Union of Ethical Societies.

[4] *Ethical Religion*, pp. 81, 84, 86, 89; for a concise treatment of this subject the reader may be referred to the present writer's *Jesus or Christ?* chapter iv.

[5] *History of European Morals*, ii., p. 26.

[6] *Op. cit.*, p. 38.

[7] *Ibid.* pp. 16-18.

[8] *Op. cit.*, p. 17.

[9] *Ibid.*, p. 57.

[10] "If for the word 'God' you read the 'universal life,'" writes the Rev. R. J. Campbell, "you have at once gained the ear of every high-minded thinking man to whom you appeal." (*The Christian Commonwealth*, April 14th, 1909.) Are we, then, to understand that if we want to appeal to high-minded thinking men, we must drop the term "God" and substitute for it, as being less offensive to these higher thinkers, some non-committal phrase like "universal life?" We say quite frankly that we are not prepared to pay such a price for making such a successful appeal; for the "universal life"—just because it is universal and all-embracing—is no more "good" than "bad"—

it has no moral character, and hence can exercise no moral authority, nor generate any moral enthusiasm.

[11] *What the Ethical Movement is*, by Harry Snell.

CHAPTER XI
PROBLEMS OF PRAYER

In the opening chapters of this book we had occasion once or twice to ask ourselves in passing how the new emphasis on the doctrine of Divine immanence was likely to affect the question of prayer; in turning now to a more direct treatment of the latter subject, this is again the first and most important query we shall have to consider. Truth, as we all know, is a "*mean*"—it represents a balance between opposing extremes; what is, however, not always recognised is that the extremes are not necessarily equidistant from the true centre, and there are cases when it is of the greatest importance to discern which of them is nearer and which more remote from the truth. In the present instance we have insisted all along that of the two possible extremes of Deism and Pantheism the former, with its exclusive insistance upon God's transcendence, is not only more intelligible but far more true than the latter, with its one-sided stress on His immanence; for, as we previously expressed it, in the exercise of religion it is the transcendent God with whom we are concerned. In fact, Deism may be a very faulty type of religion, theoretically considered; but Pantheism is religion's practical annihilation. It is not for nothing that in Persia, *e.g.*, the name of *Sufi*—in theory a pantheistic believer in the identity of the worshipper with his Deity—signifies in current use not a mystic, but a freethinker!

So far as the religious *life* is concerned, we repeat that Deism is the lesser error and the lesser danger; and nowhere is this more closely brought home to us than when we consider the reality and the meaning of prayer. For however far-off God may be thought to be, it has never been suggested that the voice of prayer is not able to travel across the distance—He may "hear us in heaven, His dwelling-place, and when He heareth, forgive;" but if His presence is so universally diffused that we ourselves form part of it, we shall hardly know to whom or to what to address ourselves in the act of adoration. We can pray to a Deity conceived as solely transcendent, but not to a Deity conceived as solely immanent, *i.e.*, as the Sum of Being. A vague "cosmic emotion" differs *toto coelo* from worship; we cannot worship that which includes us, for if we did we should be indulging in self-worship, and as for prayer, we could no more seriously offer it to the universe than to the atmosphere. This point cannot be too clearly realised. Prayer is the soul's communion with God; but if the soul is an integral constituent of God, a mode or phase of the Divine Being, then this communion, being already an accomplished and unalterable fact, cannot be so much as desired, still less does it need to be brought about by prayer or any other means whatsoever. Nothing could be more instructive in this connection than what is apparently a favourite illustration with those for whom immanence is only a synonym for Monism, and which likens the relation of God to the individual soul to that subsisting between the ocean and some individual bay: "the hundred bays and gulfs and creeks that succeed each other round the island," we read, "*are in the ocean, and the ocean is in them.*" [1] Now let us see what this means. There may be the most urgent necessity for digging channels to connect a reservoir with the sea, so that it may be filled with its fulness; but it would be absurd to speak of opening up or renewing communication between bay and ocean—a communication whose uninterrupted nature is implied in the very terms of the image. On such an interpretation of immanence, prayer in any real sense is either superfluous or impossible; for if no one hopeth for that which he seeth, neither would any one in his senses seek to bring to pass a condition of things which is thought to be already existing. Here we see once more the unbridgeable gulf between every form of "idealistic Monism"—Eastern or Western—and Christianity; for while, *e.g.*, "the central idea of Indian piety is meditation, the absorption of the individual in the life-spirit, the experience of identity with the universality and oneness of the Godhead," on the other hand "Christianity is the religion of prayer—prayer is its crown and its pearl." [2]

That is really the crux of the whole matter; prayer must be conceived as an active intercourse between the worshipper and a Person other than himself, who is the object of his worship. It is not a soliloquy—what the Germans expressively call a *Selbstgespräch*, or "self-talk"; it is not a monologue, but a dialogue; it is not a mere contemplation, but addressed to Someone who is thought of as willing to listen and able to answer. As Sabatier has well said, "*Prayer is religion in act; that is, prayer is real religion.*" Wherever men believe in a personal God, as distinct from an "all-inclusive consciousness of being" of which they are fleeting expressions—mere surface ripples on an infinite ocean—that belief will attest itself by the prayerful life. On the other hand, a prayerless religion is a contradiction in terms; it either has no needs to express or it will die from lack of self-expression. The believer will pray from a sense of inner necessity, coupled with the instinctive assurance that the need of which he is conscious will thus, and thus only, meet with its satisfaction. "The genuineness of religion"—to quote Professor William James—"is thus indissolubly bound up with the question whether the prayerful consciousness be or be not deceitful. The conviction that something is genuinely transacted in this consciousness is the very core of living religion." [3]

Is there, then, or is there not, something "genuinely transacted" in the experience of prayer? A transaction, *ex hypothesi*, can only take place between two parties; it implies two volitional centres. And, furthermore, what is it that is transacted? Is prayer only a very noble form of auto-suggestion—are its effects merely subjective, or are they also objective? These are problems which could hardly be said to exist for an earlier age; to the modern mind they are intensely real, and press for answers. It must be recognised at once that the idea of God as immanent in nature, expressing Himself in those observed uniformities to which we give the name of natural laws, creates difficulties of its own in regard to this subject; for if these laws show forth His will, is it even thinkable that our formulated desires could move Him to depart from what we might speak of as His original intention? His will is either the absolutely best or it is not; if it is, why pray that He may modify it? If it is not, is He not less than perfectly good, since His design admits of improvement? Can we conceive of Him as doing something in answer to a human petition which He would not do apart from such a petition? Can we think of Him as being prevailed upon by our assiduities and importunities to alter His decrees—is not this whole notion rather paltry and derogatory to His dignity? Everybody is familiar with these questions and arguments; let us see in what proportion truth and error are combined in them.

(1) A good deal of unnecessary difficulty arises in the first place from the habitual failure of many people to bear in mind that though God is immanent in the cosmos, He is not *only* immanent; as soon as His transcendence is realised, it is seen that there exists no *a priori* reason against the possibility of what from our point of view would look like Divine interpositions in the ordinary course of nature. We have, it must be remembered, not the slightest grounds for assuming that there can be no departures from the uniformities of nature, nor are we in a position to state dogmatically that no imaginable conditions would ever furnish an adequate reason for such a departure. Admitting that the regular processes observed in the physical universe represent something of the Divine mode of action, we have no warrant for maintaining that these are the only modes of such action; probability, in effect, is all the other way. "Lo, these are but the outskirts of His ways; and how small a whisper do we hear of Him! *But the thunder of His power who can understand?*" A transcendent God is *eo ipso* not limited to such methods as we happen to have caught a glimpse or a whisper of.

(2) But when this is clearly understood, it has on the other hand to be as frankly admitted—indeed, it is stating the obvious to say—that in modern times the idea of the uniformity of nature has obtained such a hold upon the general educated mind as renders any breach of that order far more improbable to us than it could have appeared to a pre-scientific generation. All physical science rests, broadly speaking, upon the assumption that

nature acts uniformly; without saying that it must be so, we are well assured that it is so, because all observation and experiment are found to bear out the truth of the principle we have assumed. All we have learned concerning nature excludes the notion that there is anything haphazard or arbitrary in her ways. We do not feel at all as though the action of natural forces might be suspended or modified for our particular benefit, and hence certain ideas of the efficacy of prayer—*e.g.*, for rain or fine weather—have become impossible for us to entertain with the ease of our ancestors. We start with a mental attitude—hardly to be called a prejudice, since it is based upon a large body of experience—of profound assurance that in matters like these the will of God finds its expression in the unbroken operation of His ordinary laws, "without variableness or shadow of turning"; most people, moreover, would acknowledge that it is better that these laws should be stable and capable of being learned and depended upon than that the Divine will should be incalculable—*ondoyant et divers*—a matter of moods on His side and of importunity on ours. Tennyson's familiar lines represent the typically modern outlook with the utmost accuracy and conciseness:—

God is Law, say the wise; O soul, and let us rejoice[1]
For if He thunder by law, the thunder is yet His Voice.

(3) And while the scientific temper of the present day could not fail to affect our thoughts concerning prayer in some directions, the same has surely to be said about the ethical temper of the age, as shown in our enlarged conceptions of God. To put it bluntly, much of the language about what used to be called "special providences" has become unreal and ceased to be edifying for us. On this whole subject some words of Principal Adeney's can hardly be bettered:—

Under the old theory God had His favourites who were saved by hair-breadth escapes, in accidents that were fatal to persons who were not the objects of "special providences"; this was supposed to account for the fact that one man in particular found that somebody else had taken the last berth in the ship he had meant to sail by, and so escaped the fate of the crew and passengers when it went down with all on board—no "special providence" saving them. It looks like a reflection of the pagan mythological tales about heroes rescued by the timely interference of gods and goddesses in battles where thousands of common mortals perish unheeded. It is the aristocratic idea of privilege carried up to religion. The newer view is more democratic, and it seems to agree better with our Lord's assurance that not a sparrow falls to the ground without our Father's notice, that the very hairs of our heads are all numbered.[4]

All this has its direct bearing upon the subject of prayer. We may still be occasionally regaled with stories of one solitary sailor being saved—

Providence looking after him in response to his mother's petitions—while every other soul on board was drowned; but these narratives, once irresistible in the impression they created, are to-day received with somewhat mixed feelings. The view of God's character which they inculcate is apt to strike us as unsatisfactory; that He should avert a great and presumedly unmerited physical calamity from one individual simply and solely because He has been asked to do so by some other individual, while allowing the same calamity to overtake numerous others no more deserving of affliction, does not fit in with our conception of Him. We are slowly learning to substitute for the notion of any kind of preferential treatment at the hand of God a belief in the unchanging goodness of His decrees, in the wisdom of His counsel, and in the reality of His abiding and enfolding love; by Providence we mean something that is neither local nor personal, nor particular, but universal—the Providence of unchanging law—that living and loving Will which "knoweth altogether."

(4) But if, owing to such considerations as these, we are less inclined to-day to frame certain kinds of petition, or to expect them to be answered, it is also true that we are increasingly coming to re-discover what should never have been forgotten, *viz.*, that petition is not the whole but only a part, and perhaps a subordinate part, of prayer. A glance at our Lord's priceless bequest to humanity, the Model Prayer, should suffice to place this beyond a doubt. If we study it clause by clause, we find that the first place is assigned simply to *adoration*, and the claiming of the supreme privilege of spiritual communion, with an implicit, although not explicit, *thanksgiving* for that privilege; next we find two clauses expressive of *aspiration* for the achievement of the highest aims, with the implied vow to help on their realisation by our own conduct and efforts; and not until then do we come upon a *supplication*, which moreover prays only for the simplest of material blessings—for bare sustenance, in fact. This is followed by *confession*, with a prayer for mercy, and a promise to show ourselves merciful to our brethren; and a prayer for deliverance and guidance brings us to the final act of *praise*. Thus, with one most modest exception, the blessings which God is asked to bestow are spiritual blessings; for a petition asking, *e.g.*, that the operation of some natural law may be temporarily suspended for our benefit we should look altogether in vain. In any case we ought to learn from the one prayer which our Lord expressly taught His disciples to give to mere petition a much less prominent place than it usually occupies; adoration, confession and thanksgiving should between them take the predominant share in our communion with the Most High, thus correcting the tendency to make of prayer a mere recital of wants more or less indiscriminately addressed to the Divine bounty. The supreme object to be kept in view is that we should become of God's way of thinking—not that we should attempt to make Him of ours; in Matthew Henry's shrewd

comparison, prayer is like the boat-hook, which brings the boat to the land, not the land to the boat.

But when we have clarified our ideas on the subject to this extent, we must once more face the question suggested by Professor James—*What is it that is transacted?* The effect of prayer upon those who offer it is too well-attested to be called into doubt; what we have to ask ourselves, however, is whether those effects are, in the strict sense of the term, purely "subjective," *i.e.*, as we previously expressed it, in the nature of a noble auto-suggestion. The answer to that query must in the last resort be determined by our thought concerning God and our relation to Him. Let it be said once more: if, with the pantheist, we assume that we are essentially and inalienably one with the All—part of It, as the bay is of the ocean—prayer, as the theist understands it, is a self-contradiction; if offered at all, it will be, not the establishment of a relation which is *ex hypothesi* always in being, but at most a clearer realisation by the particle of its fundamental identity with the Whole. Prayer is founded upon the belief that the Deity is at least interested in His worshipper—or else, why speak to the Unheeding? But Spinozism distinctly denies the possibility of God's entertaining any feelings towards individuals—indeed, Spinoza condemns the individual's desire for God's personal love; at most he will admit that "'God, inasmuch as He loves Himself, loves men,' because men are parts and proportions of God. . . The complacency of the Universe in its self-awareness, the love of God towards Himself, as Spinoza has it, includes us in its embrace, and that is enough." [5] We reply that this "complacency of the Universe in its self-awareness" may be enough for Spinozists; but it is not enough to move men to prayer—and this is borne out by Mr. Picton's total silence on this topic in his exposition of his Master's doctrine. Mr. Chesterton, with his usual felicity of phrase, hits the nail on the head when he says that upon this principle "the whole cosmos is only one enormously selfish person;" certainly it should be clear that on this assumption, as there can be no return of affection from a God whose love is only self-love, so the effect of prayer can only be that which is produced upon the soul by its consciousness—supposed to be elevating—of being an infinitesimal fraction of an infinite totality. We say that this consciousness is supposed to be elevating, though why it should be so is not quite apparent; for whatever this heterogeneous sum-total of existences may be, it is not, in our sense of the term, *good*, as the God of Christianity is good.

But if, instead of losing ourselves in the fog-land of Pantheism, Theosophy and their unavowed congeners, we take our stand upon the firm belief in the otherness of God, the case alters altogether. Prayer at once becomes rational instead of being a contradiction in terms; it is the accomplishment of something which is not already accomplished; it springs from the consciousness of a spiritual need, it is born of the instinct of spiritual self-preservation. It sets up a connection between two centres—man and God—which can only be connected because of a fundamental likeness subsisting between them; but the *likeness* is not *oneness*—indeed, the latter would exclude the former, for only separates can be like each other. On this theory prayer is no mere meditation, but an intense and strenuous endeavour to make actual something that is only potential; to use the simile we previously employed, it is a digging of channels along which the sea may pour of its fulness into an inland reservoir. That this is what really takes place in prayer—that there is such a real response from Him to whom it is directed—we have no hesitation whatever in affirming; and this notwithstanding the fact that such an experience cannot be proved to one who has not shared it, any more than we can convey a sense of the grandeur of Mont Blanc to one whose eye has never beheld its majestic proportions. Evidently, in this as in every corresponding case the testimony of those who say that they have had a certain experience must be preferred to that of others who can only say that they have not had it; and the witness to spiritual renewal, reinforcement, replenishing received in prayer—to the entering in of a Presence when the doors were thrown open; to a peace and blessedness which were not of the world's giving—this witness is so strong and so uniform that we have no choice but to pronounce it decisive. In every such case something had been "genuinely transacted"; not only had man spoken, but God had answered—the worshipper had not merely invoked, but in a very real sense he had evoked, the Divine Presence.

But can we go any further than this? Can we, that is to say, maintain that God answers prayer, not only by flooding the adoring soul with fresh strength, gladness, confidence, but by bringing to pass events which otherwise would not have come about? This "objective efficacy" of prayer, in the narrower sense, is frequently doubted to-day; but, as we shall attempt to show, upon grounds which, when examined, prove untenable. The difficulty, as it is most generally stated, arises from a misunderstanding; answers to prayer are regarded as interferences with the uniformities of nature, as arbitrary—and therefore unthinkable—interruptions of the chain of cause and effect, for which there can be no room in an orderly universe. This, no doubt, was what Turgenev meant when he asked, "Does not all prayer mean *au fond* a wish that in a given case two and two may not make four?" That Turgenev's aphorism quite illegitimately narrows down the meaning of prayer to petition, may pass; it is more important for us to investigate his implied challenge—the grounds upon which he expresses his absolute disbelief in the fulfilment of such petitions.[6]

A simple preliminary reflection should come to our aid. God is surely always bringing things to pass on condition that we first do certain other things, and on no other conditions whatsoever. The seeking has to go before the finding, the knocking to precede the opening of the doors. He will give us waving corn, providing the ground is ploughed and sown; that is to say, He answers our request, if we will make it in the right manner—He lays down certain rules on compliance with which we may secure certain blessings. Is it objected that ploughing and sowing, unlike prayer, are physical exertions made for the purpose of bringing about physical results? That would be a very superficial view; it is certainly truer to say that they are acts of will, and even acts of faith; and in the ultimate analysis the power which has produced the harvest is not the power of matter, but of mind—the mind of man acting in accordance with the Mind of God. Man has asked, God has answered; and would not have answered in that particular manner but for the particular manner of that request.

Let us go a step further, still keeping to the obvious. Most visitors to Geneva have made the short excursion to the *Forces matrices*, the great power-station where the swift waters of the Rhone are pressed into the service of man and made to light the streets, propel the tramways and drive all the machinery of the city. Now these vast powers were always there—no law of nature was broken, nor any new one introduced, when they were utilised to lighten man's labours and multiply his energies; all that has happened is that man has discovered existing laws and harnessed them to his use, and once more the real *force motrice* resides not in those silently-revolving engines that generate the electric current, but in the mind that devised and controls them.

Thought, then—unseen, impalpable—is energy in its essence, the master force which directs, subdues and uses matter; and in prayer we have already seen that we place ourselves in communication with the Central Force of the universe, acquiring power we should not otherwise possess, and replenishing our emptiness from an inexhaustible store. But if thought, mind, will, are that which lies behind all physical accomplishment, from the simplest to the most wonderful; and if by an exercise of the same faculty we may actually secure results of a spiritual order, direct answering messages, from God: why should it be *a priori* unthinkable that we may by the same agency of prayer obtain more "objective" responses, *viz.*, the fulfilment of our petitions? Frankly, we can discover no theoretical grounds on which such a possibility could be merely waved on one side as not worth consideration. Shall we be told that we cannot think that God would grant a certain wish only on condition that we expressed it to Him? But we have already found that in the regular experience of life the Divine bounty seems to come in response to human efforts which are ultimately efforts of the will. Once more, everything depends upon our thought of God; if He is such as Jesus taught us to regard Him, may it not well be that His Fatherly love goes out to us in fullest measure when we call upon it with fullest and most childlike trust? If it is urged that God would surely under all circumstances grant His children whatever may contribute to their happiness, we need only observe that every parent has had occasion to say to a much-loved child, "You shall have this when you know how to ask for it." The truth has been stated with characteristic simplicity and insight by Dr. James Drummond, in the words, "If God has left certain things dependent on the action of the human will, He may also have left certain things dependent on human petition." [7]

So much is sure, that in all true prayer we set spiritual forces in motion, to whose effects upon ourselves we can bear witness; and if their action in one direction is an ascertained fact, however mysterious and inexplicable, with what warrant shall we deny the possibility of their acting in another? Certainly we shall not argue that such action involves an "interference" with natural law; and if we have to admit our ignorance as to *how* such a force would operate and bring results to pass, let us remind ourselves that the ultimate "how?"—the bridge between antecedent and consequent, and why the former should be followed by the latter—always and inevitably escapes us. Why in the thousand and more observed forms of snow-crystals the filaments of ice should always be arranged at angles of 60 degrees or 120 degrees; why sulphate of potash and sulphate of alumina should crystallise in octahedrons or in cubes, but in no other forms; what is the real connection between molecular changes in the brain-substance and states of consciousness—all these, and a myriad more, are unsolved mysteries: we can only say that we are dealing with facts of experience. And as in these and countless other cases, so here also, in this matter of answers to prayer, the final and only test is that of experience. That a vessel in distress should be able to send a message to another vessel a hundred miles out of sight, and summon it to its aid, would have struck an earlier generation as a piece of wild romancing—but we know it is actually done; that a soul's earnest prayer may avail to enlist mighty energies in its help and so to bring about results which otherwise would not have come to pass, ought hardly to strike the present age as an inherently incredible proposition.

But we shall be told that our parallel does not hold good: if the Marconi apparatus failed seven times out of ten, we should hardly think it worth while to provide our ships with so unreliable an instrument; yet who would say that even three out of ten prayers for stated objects met with fulfilment? The objection, however, is not unanswerable; indeed, the very comparison employed in stating it may enable us to supply at least a partial answer. For we understand that the success of wireless messages being transmitted and received depends upon absolutely perfect "tuning"; the electric waves set up, *i.e.*, will only act upon a receiver most delicately attuned to a particular rate of oscillations, and when the difference between the rate of oscillation of the waves and the receiver exceeds one per cent., resonance ceases altogether, so that the message may be sent, but will not be received. It strikes us as hardly a fanciful supposition that many prayers fail to obtain an answer for a precisely analogous reason, *i.e.*, for lack of attuning. The mere uttering of devotional phraseology, or even the sending forth of anguished appeals, does not of necessity constitute true prayer at all, and hence remains ineffective, because the soul is not really *en rapport* with God. We suggest that the supplication which "availeth much in its working" will be the outcome of a whole spiritual discipline, whereby the individual spirit has become attuned to the Spirit whom it seeks; if the majority of prayers go unanswered, it is because they are mere recitals of a tale of wants, without even an attempt upon the part of those who utter them to put themselves into the attitude upon which an answer depends. On the other hand, where the adjustment of which we speak has reached a high state of perfection, the soul not only transmits its message to God with the perfect assurance of being heard, but it is also continually sensitive to the messages which incessantly flash through the spiritual ether from God, but which only those can hear who have learned the secret of listening for His word.

In dealing with this question of unanswered prayer, we have given the first place to what seems to us the most important as well as the least frequently regarded reason—the lack of spiritual discipline, which is ultimately the lack of faith, with which we pray. When we remember, moreover, that many of our petitions are framed in very natural and inevitable ignorance of what is for our truest good, we realise another and very obvious reason for the non-fulfilment of a large proportion of the wishes we lay before the throne of God, whose goodness is as much attested by what He denies to our foolishness as by what He grants to our entreaties. And how numerous are the prayers which reflection and an awakened moral sense rule out of court: prayers which ask God to do for us by special intervention what we ought to do for ourselves by our own effort and industry; prayer for success in dealings and enterprises which in themselves are ethically unjustifiable, and to which the only answer could be, "Thou thoughtest that I was altogether such an one as thyself"; prayers which carry the spirit of egoism, of competition, of bargaining even into our relations with the Most High; prayers of an imprecatory character such as meet and shock us in some of the psalms. How could these and their like possibly be granted by a just and merciful Creator?

But apart from such presumptuous, foolish, or impious supplications as are at once repulsed and rebuked by the Divine silence, what are the objects we may lawfully pray for, asking for a response? It must be confessed that with the exception of petitions for spiritual blessings—for a deeper faith, for a more complete obedience, for a humbler heart, for a wider sympathy—such as can never be out of place, it is impossible to draw a hard-and-fast line; there is, indeed, a whole vast category of possible objects of prayer which one cannot *a priori* pronounce legitimate or otherwise. We can only humbly confess that "we know not how to pray as we ought," nor what things it is in our best interest to have granted or withheld from us; but with this proviso, and with the clause, "Nevertheless, not my will but Thine," added to our petitions, there can be no wrong in making our requests to God for every manner of blessing, material or otherwise, and whether on our own behalf or on behalf of others. Here we may surely with all confidence and with all reverence invoke the analogy of human parenthood. No true earthly parent is offended or moved to impatience by his children expressing to him all their wants and wishes with perfect unreserve, even though his loving wisdom has anticipated their real needs, and will decide which of their desires may be granted; indeed, as we already hinted, the granting of those desires may depend to some extent upon the children's attitude, upon the filial, trustful, affectionate disposition they exhibit. So in regard to the supplications we address to our Father in Heaven: we cannot think of His being moved by our mere importunity, or by the mechanical repetition of set phrases; but that the fulfilment of some wish of ours may be conditioned by our humility and confidence in expressing it, presents no improbability. In any case, what is necessary on our part is that we should have faith, not only in God's *power* to grant our petitions, but in His *wisdom* in granting or refusing them as may be most expedient for us. We ourselves can, within limits, fulfil most of our children's requests; but a wise and loving parent will many a time say "no," when his child may marvel at what to him must seem a mere arbitrary or even unkind refusal of an innocent desire. That hapless man of genius, the late John Davidson, condensed the truth into one illuminating phrase when he spoke of prayer rightly uttered as "submissive aspiration"; it would be difficult to devise another form of words equally brief yet containing so much of the essence of the matter. Even short of actual fulfilment, it is an immeasurable privilege simply to speak to God about all the things that weigh on our minds, assured of His hearing, nor should the fact that He knows all about our troubles before we open our lips concerning them restrain our utterance; for our object is not to give Him information, but to place ourselves in conscious communion with Him, and by viewing our affairs in His light to see light.

This applies to all our petitions, and perhaps in an especial measure to intercessory prayer, those touching requests which we send up for our dear ones in sickness, peril, sorrow, need, or any other adversity. Of course, all such intercessions ought to be mentally qualified by the assurance that God will do what is best, even though we may be unable to understand His decrees; but there is nothing unreasonable in the belief that our prayers for others may be, and frequently are, directly effective, setting energies in motion which might otherwise have remained latent and inoperative. How these energies operate may be quite beyond our power to ascertain or even to guess; but if—to say it once more—the action of matter on matter, the "how" of chemical combinations, eludes us, shall we complain because the action of mind on mind, spirit on spirit, is no less elusive? The final test—whether, *e.g.*, a mother's prayer that her absent son may be preserved from the snare of some great temptation, is able to work a change in his mind—is, as we said above, the test of experience; and unless we are dogmatically determined to reject all testimony which bears on this subject, there seems no escaping the conclusion that specific prayers have been specifically, directly, and unmistakeably answered in instances too numerous to admit of explanation by coincidence.[8] The volume of human testimony bearing on this subject is too great to be swept aside by a simple refusal to consider it; if there is no insurmountable logical obstacle to the possibility of prayer proving objectively effective—and we have tried to show that there are no such obstacles—we must examine the alleged instances of such answers without prejudice; and if we do so, then, after making all legitimate deductions, we shall still find a body of residual fact which is not to be explained away.

By all means, then, we conclude, let us obey the instincts which urge us to turn to God in prayer; they lie deeper and are less fallible—embodying as they do the experience of the race—than our individual reasonings. We may tell our Father in all simplicity of whatever desires we may cherish with an approving conscience, leaving the fulfilment to His wise and steadfast love; it is not the ignorance of our requests but the faithlessness of our spirits that we most stand in need of guarding against. Let us here, as elsewhere, follow the example of the Son of God, whose unique intimacy with the Father made Him only the more earnest in communing with Him, least lonely when alone with God. Above all, let us bear in mind that the best prayer is that which has least of self-seeking in it, but is answered in the making, and so sends us back to our tasks—perhaps to our trials—refreshed as by a draught from some hidden and precious spring, renewed in manhood and nearer to God. In the oft-quoted aphorism of George Meredith, "He who rises from his prayer a better man, his prayer is answered." As a Greater than Meredith said, "Your Heavenly Father knoweth that ye have need of all these things; but seek ye first His Kingdom, and His righteousness, and all these things shall be added unto you." The ideal prayer is that which will ask little, aspire much, submit altogether; it is the soul's complete surrender to and rest in God.

[1] The Rev. E. W. Lewis, M.A., B.D., in a paper on "The Divine Immanence, its Meaning and its Implications." Compare also *The New Theology*, p. 34. As Dr. William Adamson observes, "The illustration is unfortunate. The supposed ocean is to be thought of as infinite, and the bay is finite, but in their essence and existence they are essentially one. There can be no bay where there is no boundary, and where in this case could the boundary be found, for there can be nothing outside the infinite?"

[2] Bousset, *Faith of a Modern Protestant*, p. 59.

[3] *The Varieties of Religious Experience*, p. 466.

[4] *A Century's Progress*, p. 105-6.

[5] *Spinoza*, by J. Allanson Picton, p. 213.

[6] So far, of course, as such an attitude may be the outcome of an antecedent disbelief in God, it is perfectly logical; only we have no common ground with those who take that view. It is otherwise, however, where an avowed acceptance of Theism is nevertheless accompanied by doubts as regards any objective effects flowing from supplications addressed to God; it is with such doubts as these that we are concerned.

[7] *Studies in Christian Doctrine*, p. 197.

[8] Precisely such an instance was brought under the notice of the present writer by a correspondent, whose prayers that an absent one in distant lands might be able to resist the power of strong temptation was "heard" past all doubting—and that without the object of these petitions being aware of the cause, as let a remark of his own attest: "I don't know why, but sometimes I feel myself in some way held back from doing certain things—how, I cannot explain; I only know that I should do as others do, were it not for this compelling feeling."

CHAPTER XII
IMMORTALITY

Throughout the preceding pages we have been principally engaged in tracing the effects of the idea of Divine immanence upon the main contents of religious thought. While trying to show that this idea, rightly understood and set in its proper place, embodies an important and at one time unduly neglected truth, we have also seen that its misinterpretation and over-emphasis—the tendency to view it as not only true but as constituting the whole truth—is attended by dangers of a particularly grave character. Under whatever name, idealistic Monism or any other, the doctrine which recognises only one ultimate Existence expressing itself in all things and working its will in all events, is fatal to any religion worthy the name; indeed, since the term "religion" indicates a *link*, and a link is possible only between things or beings requiring to be held together, the fundamental tenet of Monism excludes religion in the only vital sense it has ever been known to bear, and more especially the Christian religion. Quite inevitably it abandons the personality and Fatherhood of God, the selfhood and freedom of man, the reality of sin and evil, which it describes as "not-being," and the value and rationality of prayer—for how or to whom can we pray if we are already "on the eternal throne"? Quite inevitably, therefore, we may add, the votaries of this philosophy, in attempting to accommodate it to the facts of life, the intuitions of the moral self and the aspirations of the soul, are faced everywhere by irreconcilable antinomies and "find no end, in wandering mazes lost."

Are the assumptions of the monist any more in harmony with the doctrine of immortality than with those other beliefs with which it thus finds itself at variance? We have already seen that they are not: neither the Monism of Mr. Picton nor that of Mr. Wells leaves any room for personal survival—as is, indeed, only to be expected in accordance with their premises; for if the individual as such does not really exist, why should he persist? And from yet another monistic quarter we are oracularly assured that we shall "one day know that the end of our being is that it may *be submerged without reserve in the infinite ocean of God*." Nothing could be more definite; nor, it must be confessed, more utterly hopeless. To be "submerged without reserve" is to cease from even the illusion of individuality; it is absorption, Nirvana.

In taking up this position, in finally quenching

> The hope whereto so passionately cling
> The dreaming generations from of old,

the monist is merely true to his creed; we may, however, express a preference that he should do so without religious circumlocutions—that the verdict should be, as in the famous historical instance, "*la mort, sans phrase.*" When Mr. Wells says—

I do not believe I have any personal immortality. . . The experiment will be over, the rinsed beaker returned to its shelf, the crystals gone dissolving down the wastepipe—[1]

we know where we are, and feel thankful to the author for his frankness; to talk about submersion in "the infinite ocean of God," on the other hand, invests an idea which, nakedly stated, means annihilation pure and simple, with a pseudo-religious air which is far more subtly dangerous. Indeed, of the various expedients for extinguishing men's faith in the life to come, this is probably the most insidiously effective in use to-day; it is the silken handkerchief, drenched with chloroform and held quite gently to the victim's face—a lethal weapon in all but appearance. And there are some who are attracted by the faint, cloying odour of this chloroform.

Before we examine this fashionable doctrine of absorption, however, it may be well to deal with certain other causes which between them account for much of the uneasiness—often unavowed but nevertheless very real—concerning a future life, which unquestionably is widely felt in our day. All assertions to the contrary notwithstanding, it is a case of uneasiness, and not of indifference; the bravado which professes to give thanks to "whatever gods there be"—

That no life lives for ever
That dead men rise up never,
That even the weariest river
  Winds somewhere safe to sea—

convinces no one. Most men have known moods of severe depression and lassitude when not to be at all seemed the one consummation to be desired; but that is not the normal attitude of normal people. Such would still fain believe that the grave is not the end, but many of them are in a state of bewilderment and insecurity. On the one hand men have never grown reconciled to the heart-breaking triviality of death, never accepted this dispensation without a question, a hope, or, failing hope, a sense of rebellion; on the other, we have to recognise that we live in an age when multitudes have ceased to accept religious beliefs simply upon the authority of the Bible—when educated people generally have come quite definitely to disbelieve in the resurrection of the body, a final day of judgment, a localised heaven and material hell—an age which must be one of manifold doubts and misgivings.

But this break-up of Biblical authority and its unquestioning acceptance is itself largely due to that resistless advance of physical science which has reconstructed the world for us with such masterful hands. The results of the modern conception of the universe are only just beginning to get into our system; as yet they are still largely unassimilated, and give us trouble accordingly. Let us take such a statement as the following, and imagine its effect upon the average individual:—

Think of Mercury in its wild rush through the solar heat, or Venus gleaming in the western sky, or ruddy Mars with its tantalising problems, or of mighty Jupiter 1,230 times the size of our own planet, or of Saturn with its wondrous rings, or of Uranus and Neptune revolving in their tremendous orbits—the latter nearly three thousand millions of miles away from the centre of our system. . . But the true awfulness is yet untouched. What of the millions of millions of suns that blaze in immeasurable space beyond our comparatively little solar sphere? Sirius alone, at the foot of the constellation of Orion, is 125 times larger than our sun. Fifteen hundred millions of millions of miles away, where ordinary eyes dimly descry half a dozen points of light, the telescope reveals more than a thousand orbs, some seventy of them vaster than our sun. What indeed is the whole of this our tiny planet compared with Alcyone—1,000 times larger than our central sun![2]

These, of course, are among the commonplaces of modern astronomy; but we do not think we are wrong in saying that they leave a great many minds singularly ill at ease, in a condition of vague but unmistakeable discomfort, oppressed by the vastness of the universe as revealed by science, feeling lost and utterly insignificant in this illimitable expanse of worlds on circling worlds, and aeons upon exhaustless aeons. It was possible, when the universe was regarded as a comparatively small affair, with our earth as its veritable centre, to think oneself of sufficient value in the scheme of things to live for ever; but now such a claim seems to not a few grotesque in its presumption. Have we not been told by Mr. Balfour that, so far as natural science by itself is able to teach us, man's "very existence is an accident, his story a brief and discreditable episode in the life of one of the meanest of the planets"?—and shall such a one, member of such a race, dream of prolonging his atomic existence world without end? As Lucretius asked:—

What! Shall the dateless worlds to dust be blown
Back to the unremembered and unknown,
  And this frail Thou—this flame of yesterday—
Burn on, forlorn, immortal, and alone?

This mental attitude, familiar enough nowadays, has been forcibly and typically expressed in a clever, melancholy book, *The Letters Which never*

Reached Him. "We suffer," the author says, "from our own diminutiveness and from the narrow limits of our life and knowledge since the endlessness of space and time have been taught to us. People of former epochs cannot have known this contrast between human smallness and the world's infinity; they must have been more contented, because they fancied they were made in right proportion to everything else." Such conditions as these favoured the flourishing of "that highest blossom of the conviction of personal importance, the belief in one's eternal individual continuance." "But one who has been cast by the waves on countless foreign shores, and who has reflected that everywhere, and since times infinite, millions and millions have been born and buried without leaving by their coming and going more trace than the swarms of insects which for a moment glide through the rays of the sun—such a one loses the belief in the importance of all transitory phases, and doubts the inner necessity of an eternal continuance for all those ephemeral, ant-like existences which in endless, unchanging repetitions ever rise anew to disappear again." Modern astronomy and geology, by expanding the world beyond all conception, seem, in fact, but to emphasise Omar Khayyam's mocking lines:—

And fear not lest Existence, closing your
Account and mine, should know the like no more;
  The Eternal Saki from that bowl hath pour'd
Millions of Bubbles like us, and will pour.

And if such are the reflections forced upon us by the contemplation of the vastness of the cosmos—a vastness in whose midst we feel homeless and forlorn—it has further to be remembered that the attitude of modern science, as embodied in that of some of its most confident and popular representatives, has been distinctly and openly unfavourable to belief in a future life. If man was truly descended from the lower creation, it seemed obvious to infer that as had been his origin, so also would be his destiny—the destiny of the beasts that perish. The *Kraft und Stoff* school of physicists proclaimed aloud that consciousness was only a function of the brain, and would come to a stop together with the mechanism which produced it; as Haeckel expressed it, "The various functions of the soul are bound up with certain special parts of the brain, and cannot be exercised unless these are in a normal condition; if the areas are destroyed their function is extinguished; and this is especially applicable to the 'organs of thought,' the four central instruments of mental activity." [3] But if our inner life was merely the counterpart of certain changes in the grey matter of the brain, how could the function be expected to persist after its organ had undergone decay?

Such, in short, are our principal modern difficulties with regard to belief in a life to come; do they, or do they not, present valid and insuperable obstacles to a reasonable faith?

(1) While making all allowance for the feeling of insignificance and forlornness which is apt to overwhelm us when we begin to realise the immensity of the material universe, a little closer thought should make it obvious that nothing in the nature of mere bulk or bigness furnishes even a reasonable presumption, let alone a convincing argument, against the survival of the soul; it is indeed difficult to perceive what legitimate bearing these physical phenomena are supposed to have upon a purely spiritual question. If we are to argue on *a priori* grounds, we are on the contrary justified in saying that the human mind, which has discovered and is capable of co-ordinating the myriad facts concerning the world of matter that make up modern science, is itself something far more wonderful than any of its discoveries, or the sum of them. If we are asked, "Is it conceivable that suns and stars shall pass away—as they undoubtedly will—and that man shall persist?" we can but answer, "Yes; it is very conceivable; for man is far more highly organised than suns and stars, moves on an immeasurably higher level, can reason, look before and after, form ideals of conduct, reach out in love, and think the thoughts of God after Him." As soon as we leave the lower reaches of being, bulk is seen to matter very little. The immense proportions of those flying reptiles and other monsters which peopled the earth in pre-historic times did not protect them against dying out, and their places being taken by much slighter creatures which had some more valuable attributes than size; the *diplodocus Carnegii* in the British Museum measures some seventy-five feet, but that fact did not prevent the species from becoming extinct uncounted ages since—simply because it was lacking in the higher qualities which would have enabled it to survive. And even the *diplodocus*, with its lumbering body and diminutive brain, was whole worlds superior to inorganic nature. That the marvellous thing called human personality should outlast the decay of what is so much inferior to itself, is therefore not only not inconceivable, but in itself not even improbable. It is a strange sort of modesty—to say the least of it—which would make us think ourselves of less account in the scale of existence or the sight of God than unconscious matter in its cruder and lower stages. One might as sensibly urge that the delicate hairspring of a watch, being of featherweight and almost invisible, must be worth less than a lump of crude iron-ore.

(2) We turn to the supposed argument from evolution, *viz.*, from man's lowly origin, as furnishing a strong presumption against his immortality. This plea, familiar enough in sceptical discussions of the subject, has been put forward with great poetic force by Mr. William Watson; after graphically describing "the gibbering form obscene that was and was not

man," as lower in many respects than the beasts and birds in whose midst he dwelt, he suggests that it was

> Rather some random throw
>   Of heedless Nature's die,
> 'Twould seem, that from so low
>   Hath lifted man so high.
> If, then, our rise from gloom
>   Hath this capricious air,
> What ground is mine to assume
>   An upward process there,
> In yonder worlds that shine
>   From upward tracts of sky?
> No ground to assume is mine
>   Nor warrant to deny.
> Equal, my source of hope, my reason for despair.

But, with great admiration for Mr. Watson as a poet, it is impossible not to recognise that at least two radical flaws lurk in his agnostic argument. In the first place, he makes the mistake of judging issues by origins instead of origins by issues; the sub-human beginnings of man trouble us not at all, since we can see in the subsequent history of the race how great were the possibilities infolded in that "gibbering form obscene," and unfolded in a Plato, a Raphael, a Shakespeare. That such a development from such a lowly initial stage should have been so much as possible, is in itself significant of much; for nothing is evolved that was not first involved. But in the second place, Mr. Watson's assumption that the process which lifted man from the level of the brute to one immeasurably higher was dictated by "hap and hazard" strikes us as wholly gratuitous. On the face of it, that process, in itself so little to be expected, bears the mark, not of chance but of its very contrary. That the cosmic drama should have followed this particular course; that from the cooling down of fiery nebulas there should have come forth the orderly system we behold in nature; that life should have climbed up from the speck of protoplasm "through primal ooze and slime," making its way step by step through all the lower creation until it "blossomed into man"—this, to the unbiassed mind, does not wear the aspect of mere incalculable accident, but of all-embracing wisdom and directivity. And once we have shaken off the delusion that the marvellous order and progress we behold in nature are the outcome of chance, we have the best of reasons for assuming that the same "upward process" will still continue, reaching forward from the seen to the unseen; at any rate, so well-qualified and thorough-going an evolutionist as Professor Fiske gave it as his mature opinion that "in the course of evolution there is no more philosophical difficulty in man's acquiring immortal life, than in his acquiring the erect posture and articulate speech." [4]

And the reasonableness of this view grows the clearer to us the more we realise the purposive character of the evolutionary process. The unmistakeable purpose of that process is the production of the higher from the lower; all through the ages the vast design works itself out in a ceaseless ascending movement, the theme expanding, its meaning becoming more apparent. Then, when a certain point in this development has been reached, evolution takes a direction such as no one could have forecast: "its operation upon the physical frame is diverted to the mind, the centre of interest transferred from the outward organism to the inner forces of which it is the vehicle"—and man becomes a living soul. Since, then, it has taken all these myriad ages, all this immense expenditure of planning and energy, to produce what is incontestably the crowning work of creation on this globe, must we not say that this was the issue towards which the whole process was set in motion from the very beginning? And if this is so, are we to think that at the end, when its carefully, patiently wrought-out purpose has been attained, this process suddenly turns irrational, and hands over its last and highest product to destruction? As has been well said, "To suppose that what has been evolved at such cost will suddenly collapse, is to suppose that the whole scheme of things is self-stultifying"; and for such a supposition we see not only no necessity, but no shadow of warrant.

The question is reduced to this: are man's highest spiritual qualities, into the production of which all this creative energy has gone, to disappear with the rest? Has all this work been done for nothing? Is it all ephemeral, all a bubble that bursts, a vision that fades? Are we to regard the Creator's work as like that of a child, who builds houses out of blocks, just for the pleasure of knocking them down? For aught that science can tell us, it may be so, but I can see no good reason for believing any such thing . . . The more thoroughly we comprehend that process of evolution by which things have come to be what they are, the more we are likely to feel that to deny the everlasting persistence of the spiritual element in man is to rob the whole process of its meaning. It goes far towards putting us to permanent intellectual confusion, and I do not see that anyone has as yet alleged, or is ever likely to allege, a sufficient reason for our accepting so dire an alternative.[5]

If belief in the soul's persistence must always be an act of faith, it is for the evolutionist an act of reasonable faith, based on his experience of the rationality, and what has been called the integrity, of the cosmos.

(3) Of the hostility of physical science to belief in life beyond the grave it is perhaps sufficient to say that the somewhat dogmatic attitude of denial

which flourished in certain scientific circles somewhere about a quarter of a century ago has to-day made room for a very different temper, at once more sympathetic and more willing to acknowledge that a belief is not necessarily disproved because the methods of the chemical or biological laboratory fail to substantiate it. As for the crude proposition that the brain secretes thought as the liver secretes bile, and that the life of the soul must cease with that of the body, this was characterised by the eminent thinker whom we quoted a moment ago as "perhaps the most colossal instance of baseless assumption that is known to the history of philosophy." Admitting that to every state of consciousness, to every minutest transition in our thoughts, there corresponds a cerebral change, it is yet nothing less than a childish blunder to confound correspondence with causality. The materialist has positively no good ground for stating that cerebral changes are the *causes* of the mental states corresponding to them; indeed, the contrary proposition is far more inherently probable, since it is spirit, and not matter, that "possesses the power of purpose," and may therefore be regarded as the final cause of matter.[6] When Professor Haeckel urges that "the various functions of the soul are bound up with certain special parts of the brain," and cease when the latter are destroyed, the reply is quite simple: *non sequitur.* He has apparently forgotten his own warning against the "dangerous error" of a "one-sided over-estimation of experience." [7] The utmost that experience can prove is that the brain is the transmitting apparatus for flashing forth and making intelligible the messages of the soul, and that, when this apparatus breaks down, further transmission of messages becomes impossible; but no experience can prove that when the instrument is destroyed, the soul which used it for purposes of communication and self-manifestation ceases to be, and only slipshod logic would draw such an inference. In discussing the Divine Personality, we already quoted Mill, a far more careful reasoner than Haeckel, who laid it down that while experience furnished us with no example of any series of states of consciousness without a material brain, yet it was "as easy to imagine such a series of states without as with this accompaniment"; indeed, he saw no valid reason to preclude us from supposing that "the same thoughts, emotions, volitions, and even sensations which we have here, may persist or recommence somewhere else under other conditions"—*i.e.*, without such an apparatus as is at present at our disposal. It is only a dogmatic materialist of Haeckel's almost extinct pattern who could fail to make the simple distinction between visible instrument and invisible player.

Turning aside, however, from the antiquated views of Haeckel—views which, as he himself bitterly complains, some of his most illustrious scientific compeers in his own country, men like Virchow, Du Bois-Reymond and Wundt lived to repudiate[8]—we may for a moment glance at an argument on behalf of belief brought forward by so distinguished and modern a spokesman of physical science as Sir Oliver Lodge. His contention, set forth in the course of a paper on *The Permanence of Personality*,[9] is really identical with that which Browning expresses with such passionate conviction in the words, "There shall never be one lost good." While we have become familiar with such a conception as the conservation of energy, Sir Oliver Lodge brings before us Professor Höffding's axiom of the "conservation of value," and applies it to the question under discussion. According to him, "the whole progress and course of evolution is to increase and intensify the Valuable—that which 'avails' or is serviceable for highest purposes"; and he accordingly defines immortality as the persistence of things which the universe has gained and which, once acquired, cannot be let go. "From this point of view," he says, "the law of evolution is that Good shall on the whole increase in the universe with the process of the suns: that immortality itself is a special case of a more general law, namely, that in the whole universe nothing really finally perishes that is worth keeping, that a thing once attained is not thrown away." The soul, in other words, will not perish—just as we had already argued—because it is too valuable to perish; if we may trust this latest interpretation of the meaning and purpose of evolution, the spiritual element in man will endure because it is worthy to endure.

But how are we to think of its enduring? As a separate self, conscious of its identity, able to form the proposition "I am I," or swallowed up in the Whole, with a final merging and loss of selfhood? Must we think of man's ultimate destiny in the terms of the concluding distichs of Mr. Watson's great *Hymn to the Sea*—a consummation

> When, from this threshold of being, these steps of the
>   Presence, this precinct,
> Into the matrix of Life darkly divinely resumed,
> Man and his littleness perish, erased like an error
>   and cancelled,
> Man and his greatness survive, lost in the greatness
>   of God?

That is the query with which we opened this chapter; and, in answering it, it is but fair to say that Sir Oliver Lodge shows a marked inclination to take up a position identical with that of Mr. Watson: "Everything sufficiently valuable," he says, "be it beauty, artistic achievement, knowledge, unselfish affection, may be thought of as enduring henceforth and for ever, *if not with an individual and personal existence, yet as part of the eternal Being of God.*"

Now this is not only a wholly unsatisfactory conclusion from the point of view of religion; it is a surrender of the very point at issue—*viz.*, the permanence of personality—and in reality lets slip what Sir Oliver Lodge himself was contending for. It is unsatisfactory from the point of view of religion; for such a re-absorption of the soul into a "grand self-conscious totality of being," involving of necessity the end of all we mean by individuality, consciousness, character, is not immortality at all—to all intents and purposes it is, as we said, annihilation. There is not an iota to choose, so far as the religious believer is concerned, between this theory and the frank materialism of Lucretius, so wonderfully rendered by Mr. Mallock:—

> The seeds that once were we take flight and fly,
> Winnowed to earth, or whirled along the sky,
>   Not lost but disunited. *Life lives on.*
> *It is the lives, the lives, the lives that die.*
>
> They go beyond recapture and recall,
> Lost in the all-indissoluble All:
>   Gone like the rainbow from the fountain's foam,
> Gone like the spindrift shuddering down the squall,
>
> Flakes of the water, on the waters cease!
> Soul of the body, melt and sleep like these.
>   Atoms to atoms—weariness to rest—
> Ashes to ashes—hopes and fears to peace!

Pantheism may speak delusively of "the peace of absorption in the Infinite," or of the end of our being as submersion, "without reserve, in the infinite ocean of God"; but regarded from the standpoint of individuality, there is no difference between such a fate and the total extinction of the soul—

> The healing gospel of the eternal death

—preached with such haunting eloquence by the Roman poet. The truth, as Dr. Illingworth has well expressed it, is that in practice "Pantheism is really indistinguishable from Materialism; it is merely Materialism grown sentimental, but no more tenable for its change of name." [10]

But, in the next place, in tentatively committing himself to the conclusion we are criticising, it seems to us that Sir Oliver Lodge loses sight of the very essence of his own contention: his conclusion, in effect, contradicts his premises. Syllogistically, and, of course, very bluntly stated, his argument might be summed up as follows: "What is of value is preserved; the soul is of value; therefore the soul is—dissolved." Let us put this a little more explicitly. That which has been gained in the course of evolution, so far as the human soul is concerned—that which makes it worthy to endure, *viz.*, its character, conscience, idealism and so forth—belongs to the soul precisely as an individual entity, and in no other way whatsoever; neither can it be effectively preserved save in the form of an individual entity. The soul, in other words, is not to be compared to a mere quantum of raw material, or to a cupful of water temporarily drawn from an infinite deep into which it may be poured back, and nothing lost: it is, on the contrary, a highly individualised product, so individual as to be unique, and in simply being merged in the totality of being all that is most valuable in it would be lost and wasted. We have no difficulty in believing that mere *life*—the potentiality, the material out of which higher things evolve—may go back into the all, to arise again in new manifestations and combinations; but it is otherwise with the highly complex resultant of the evolutionary process which we call *personality*, endowed as it is with self-consciousness, with the sense of right and wrong, the capacity for ideals, the faculty of self-giving, a god-like within answering to the God without. It is because these things—those which "avail for highest purposes"—make man personal and mark him off, broadly speaking, from the lower, sub-human life out of which he has emerged, that we believe in the permanence of human personality, of the spiritual element in man, in the survival of the soul *as individual and personal*, and not merely as "part of the eternal Being of God." A simple illustration will help us to enforce our point of view. In the process of porcelain manufacture the half-finished ware is placed in "seggars" or coarse clay shells for protection in the glaze or enamel kiln. These temporary shells, having served their purpose, are broken up and ground down again into a shapeless mass under heavy revolving rollers; but no one would dream of treating the graceful vases and figures they enclosed for a time after the same fashion. The parallel is fairly obvious: the protecting clay envelope broken to pieces, merged and mingled with other clay, to be so used and broken a hundred times; the precious product carefully taken from its coarse shell and preserved. The dust returns to the earth as it was, and the spirit returns unto God who gave it: returns, but not as it came forth from Him, but differentiated, individual, shaped and coloured; returns, not to be absorbed and lost in an "all-indissoluble All," but, as we hold, for still further processes of perfecting.

And if we are asked for the ground whence we derive the latter assurance, we answer, It is founded upon our belief, not in a "universal substance" or an "all-inclusive consciousness of being," but in the God and Father of our Lord Jesus Christ. By no possibility can these two conceptions be made to harmonise or to pass into one another; on the former view, as we have seen, the significance of the individual soul is and must be *nil*—on the latter, the value of the soul is infinite, because it is the object of the Divine Love, created by God "unto Himself," in order to experience and respond to His affection. On the former view, we are finite modes of infinite Being—on the latter, we are children of the Father.

It is because we have believed the love which God hath to us—the love made manifest supremely in Jesus Christ—that we echo so confidently the poet's "Thou wilt not leave us in the dust": the Christian doctrine of immortality flows quite naturally from the Christian doctrine of God. The argument is frankly ethical; it flows from the view of God's character which we have received through the revelation of that character in His Son. Without hurling any wild indictment at life, we dare to say that it requires to be supplemented by the life to come in order to fit in with the idea of a just and loving God, a faithful and merciful Creator. This span of days, this hand's-breadth of existence, is too palpably fragmentary. The sinner, the failure, all those who have here missed the way, ask another opportunity of the Divine mercy; the wronged, the sufferers from unmerited griefs, those whose lives passed in gloom and closed in tragedy, appeal for justice; the longing for reunion with loved ones whose going hence has left us permanently poorer, demands fulfilment; the goodness of the good and the sanctity of the saint plead for "the wages of going on." This ethical argument for personal immortality—Browning's "On the earth the broken arcs; in the heaven the perfect round"—will carry no weight with those who profess a "religion of the universe"; for the universe, viewed simply as the sum-total of phenomena, possesses, as we have so frequently pointed out, no sufficiently decided moral character to inspire us with confidence in its justice, or mercy, or pitifulness. On the other hand, the same argument will powerfully appeal to all who believe in the Divine Goodness, and especially to those who, looking unto Jesus, have in His face beheld the lineaments of the Father. If God be such as Jesus taught, then life everlasting may be a dim, intangible dream, but a dream that is destined to come true: we shall be satisfied when we awake.

Thus, at the close of this inquiry, we find ourselves left with two ultimate realities—two, not one; alike, not identical; related, and *therefore* distinct, for a relation can only subsist between one and another: the realities of God and the soul. *Gott und die Seele, die Seele und ihr Gott*—these two, eternally akin, yet in their kinship unconfounded, make up the theme and the content of religion; and any attempt to obliterate the distinction between them in some monistic formula, any tendency to surrender either the Divine or the human personality, any philosophy which seeks to merge man in God and God in the universe, is fatal to religion itself. We have been told of late that "there is no Divine immanence which does not imply the allness of God"; we reply that there is no sane and sober theology which will not feel called upon to challenge this fundamental error. God, immanent in the universe as life and energy, is not the universe; man, the partaker of the Divine nature, indwelt by the Spirit of God, is other than God. These are commonplaces, truly; yet in the presence of more than one contemporary movement aiming to set these basal truths aside—truths whose acceptance or rejection involves far-reaching issues in faith and morals—there may be some excuse and even some necessity for reiterating them so persistently and at such length as has been done in these pages.

Man is inalienably akin to God—man is everlastingly other than God; upon this note we are content to close. In that fact we have, not only the ultimate explanation of the phenomenon of religion, the ultimate foundation of ethics, the ultimate ground of the felt need of salvation, but also the ultimate hope of immortality—that reasonable hope, expressed by the Hebrew seer for all time in words of sublime and intuitive insight: *Art not THOU from everlasting, O Lord my God, mine Holy One?* WE SHALL NOT DIE.

[1] *First and Last Things*, pp. 80, 238.

[2] Ballard, *Christian Essentials*, pp. 10-12.

[3] *The Riddle of the Universe*, p. 72.

[4] *Life Everlasting*, p. 85. To the same effect is Huxley's statement declaring that while he would "neither affirm nor deny the immortality of man," immortality itself struck him "*as not half so wonderful as the conservation of force or the indestructibility of matter.*"

[5] *Man's Destiny*, by John Fiske, pp. 114-116.

[6] Cp. Illingworth, *Divine Immanence*, p. 8.

[7] *The Riddle of the Universe*, p. 7.

[8] *Op. cit.*; see ch. vi., *passim*.

[9] See the *Hibbert Journal*, April 1908, pp. 565-567.

[10] *Divine Immanence*, p. 39.

Milton Keynes UK
Ingram Content Group UK Ltd.
UKHW030625061024
449204UK00004B/307